ROTI

ROTI

90 simple recipes for the Indian bread and its accompaniments

Anuradha Ravindranath

DK

Contents

GETTING STARTED

The making of *Roti*

Roti kha kar jaana – if asked for a phrase that encapsulates the era I grew up in, I would quote this one. Unpretentious, earthy, and direct, as an invitation to "stay and eat with us", it captures the warm sociability of a time when hospitality resided in homes – gracious homes, big and small. It was where families and friends ate and celebrated together, where friends of friends were always welcome; where people stopped by to visit at all times of the day and were always expected to stay for a meal – not tea and biscuits – but a meal. If you arrived late morning, you stayed for lunch, if you arrived early evening, then you stayed for dinner, and if it happened to be somewhere in between and you just could not stay that long, then the delicacies served often surpassed a meal.

I was born in 1953, just six years after India became an independent country. Our home was on 6 Aurangzeb Road in New Delhi and my earliest memories of it are of playing in its little garden with my father and the family dog, Zulu. There was plenty of family on both my parents' side and people were in and out of our house all the time, lucky to be alive, and just glad to be together. I was very young, but I have strong memories of happy times as part of a small family. Another, somewhat hazy, memory leads me to believe that the exceptional quality of our dining table goes back to those days in the cottage. We had a cook named Sudama, and, while I do not remember his daily fare, I can still taste the baked apples and caramel lace basket he used to make. Even in the early 1960s, everything was still quite British – especially the food department of our home.

My father, whom we addressed as Bapu, was the great-grandson of Sir Gangaram, the renowned civil engineer and architect celebrated for his urban work in Lahore (in present-day Pakistan). Bapu grew up in undivided India, in a joint family in Lahore. His love for food and cooking, as I gathered from the stories he shared, developed from watching the cooks go about their daily business of preparing the most delicious meals for what must have been more than 20 to 25 family members, in addition to the large floating population of friends and work acquaintances. Bapu had a privileged view – the cook would lift and settle him securely on his shoulders whenever the little boy came into the kitchen. When Bapu turned 11, he was sent to Doon School, a boarding school in the foothills of the Siwaliks (in the present-day state of Uttarakhand in India). After completing his schooling, he returned to Lahore, where he finished college – it was a good life.

Politically, however, things were not going well. With independence came the Partition of India in

Sudama with the author's brother Lakshman

The author's parents, Ranjit and Kamala Rai in 1949

1947. Caught in the rioting that tore the subcontinent apart, friends advised Bapu to leave before the borders closed. Lahore was not safe, no longer home. Friends and even those considered extended family became strangers and, like many others, he arrived in Delhi with nothing in hand.

My mother's family was from Karachi, also part of undivided India. Her progressive and liberal father sent her to a university town called Santiniketan, near Calcutta (now Kolkata) in West Bengal, where his brother was a teacher for higher education. On her return, she taught at Ganga High School for girls in Lahore. Despite skirmishes that hinted at the violence that Partition might bring, she decided to visit Delhi on 14 August 1947, to be there at midnight when the first prime minister, Jawaharlal Nehru, announced India's independence. Expecting to be back in Lahore shortly thereafter, all she brought with her was an overnight bag. But, as rioting escalated to carnage, the borders were sealed. There was no going back – no option but to remain in Delhi with the sister of a friend from Santiniketan. She was 26 years old and, though she lived to be 96, she never did go back to the land of her birth.

Never one to sit idle if she could help it, she volunteered to work at Kingsway Camp in the old city of Delhi, one of the many camps set up to house those displaced by Partition. One day, when she had been delayed at the camp, her friend arranged a car through a family connection to take them home. My father was driving the car. As it was past curfew, the camp had provided them with an armed guard. It did not occur to anyone to ascertain if the gun was capped, and so when my father had to brake abruptly, the gun went off. The bullet went through my mother's arm. With blood streaming and panic rising, she was rushed to the already overflowing Wellington Hospital. Her arm was stitched up, without anaesthesia, and she was kept in hospital for observation. My father visited her every day and the rest, as they say, is history. They were married in 1949.

Even though they came from wealth, neither of them had very much at the time – what they did have was family. Bapu's aunt (his father's sister) was living in one of the spacious bungalows on Aurangzeb Road. She offered the newlyweds a little outhouse within the compound to set up home and start their life together. That is where I was born.

GETTING THE RIGHT INGREDIENTS

By the winter of 1957, we were well settled in "the cottage". Our beloved Zulu had died and to fill the gap, my brother and I took to feeding a stray, whom we named Jimmy.

The author with Jimmy and little Frosty in 1964

Jimmy was wilful. However much we tried, he would eat his fill and go away. Bapu and I followed him one morning and found him trotting through the gates of the sprawling bungalow No. 3 on Prithviraj Road. It was obvious that the beautiful house was unoccupied. We wandered around till we spotted a *chowkidar* (a guard or watchman). One thing led to another and, in June 1958, Bapu raised enough money to buy the property from the owner, the Maharani of Tehri Garhwal. We moved in with Jimmy soon after.

No. 3 was a typical bungalow in the newly developed capital of New Delhi, designed by the British architect Sir Edwin Lutyens. The one-acre plot had lawns in the front and on both the sides. The walls were thick and retained heat in winter. In summer, the central open courtyard pushed the air to circulate freely through rooms that had plenty of windows and cooled the house down. There were no water heaters or air conditioners.

The kitchen, too, did not have any fancy gadgets. Cooking was done on coal *chulhas* (traditional Indian stoves) set in brickwork. Since cooking was slow and went on for most part of the day, they retained heat through the day. To take advantage of this, a cast iron box with a door was set in the middle. Surrounded by *chulhas*, it worked like an oven, in which it was possible to bake desserts. I particularly remember relishing the most delicious *nan*

The author's childhood home
at No. 3, Prithviraj Road

khatais (similar to shortbread) that emerged from it. It was after we came to No. 3 that my father truly came into his own and took over the kitchen. This may have been due to the fact that my mother suffered a major loss of sensation in her arm from nerve damage caused by the shooting incident, which prevented her from taking on many domestic responsibilities. But that notwithstanding, what I do know for a fact is that Bapu enjoyed good food – discovering it, preparing it, and serving it.

As the years went by, I realized the importance of our dining table – how focal it was in building ties between family and friends. Every day there would be more than 8 to 10 members of the family sharing a meal, even though we were no longer a joint family. Various aunts and uncles, cousins of all ages and their friends, were urged *roti khake kar jana*. This was not just in our home. Hospitality came from the heart and was generously extended in all homes regardless of the size of kitchen or how well-to-do the family was.

THE PROCESS OF KNEADING

I was a sickly, cranky child who disliked eating and fussed about everything. I had to be begged, wheedled, and forced to even put a morsel in my mouth. Fortunately, Mai was there for me. She was from the hills of Himachal Pradesh and had made her home with us. Her name was Krishna but, though she was not old, everyone called her Mai (literally, "mother" but also used as a term of respect). She knew I fussed about everything related to food and had her own way of getting me to eat.

My father was passionate about growing uncommon vegetables and had planted many fruit trees as well as a grapevine. Much before leafy greens became a fad, our kitchen garden produced all kinds of *saag* (leafy green vegetables). Mai would take me around the garden to help her pluck whatever greens she could lay her hands on, including grape leaves, which I never imagined could be eaten. She would wash them before coarsely chopping them, while I watched fascinated. She would then take five or six handfuls of atta in a *parat* (a steel basin often used in Indian kitchens to mix atta), add a pinch of salt and some water, then start kneading. In the blink of an eye, or so it seemed to me then, the dough was ready.

Next, a kadhai (Indian wok) would go on one *chulha* and a tava (Indian griddle for making rotis) on the other. She would pour mustard oil into the kadhai, followed by a couple of minced garlic cloves, chopped tomatoes, salt, turmeric – nothing was measured, it was all instinct – and finally the greens. Everything was stirred, covered, and left to cook as I watched transfixed.

She would then roll out the dough – it yielded no more than 4 rotis, almost 22cm (9in) in diameter and 2–3mm (about ⅛in) thick – which she roasted on the tava. The cooking may have taken 20 to 25 minutes, but I was never bored. She spoke incessantly as she cooked, giving me all sorts of instructions that I still follow,

"Washing greens is important as the leaves have dust particles and who knows what's on them, even if you can't see them."

"Heat mustard oil but not till it smokes."

"Minced garlic releases aromas quickly."

She would place one, well-cooked roti, with ghee spread liberally over it, and a helping of greens on a plate for me and serve herself the same. We would sit on the floor by the kitchen doorway and as we ate, she would tell me about her life in the village. I, who did not like eating, would finish all that was on my plate without even noticing. This ritual lasted till I went to boarding school at the age of 11, and to this day, I can affirm that those were the best rotis I have ever eaten – flavourful and imbued with love, patience, and understanding.

Some enjoy boarding school, some do not, but one thing is certain – all boarders learn to appreciate food as they are pretty much starving, or so it seems, throughout the day.

The author with Mai just before her retirement in 1994

I was away for only two and a half years, but the experience changed me. Once home, I started taking an interest in food, and not just in eating. I noticed how passionate my father was about cuisines from across India and the world, which he explored during his travels for work.

Every evening, after work, he would come home with bags full of ingredients for that day's experiment. I would watch him cook, listening as he imparted tips, just as Mai had done.

"The best result is when the ingredients are also of the purest quality."

"Ghee is most beneficial for health and perfect Indian food flavour."

"The best stock is home-made, both vegetarian and non-vegetarian."

"Herbs should always be used fresh."

"Rotis taste best when eaten hot off the tava."

RESTING AND ROLLING

Once I started paying attention, there was so much to notice – how the changing seasons influenced what was served at the table. The vegetables varied, as did the staple. As winter approached, everyone looked forward to sitting in the sun, enjoying bajre ki roti with makkhan (pearl millet flatbread with butter) or makki ki roti with sarson ka saag (cornmeal flatbread with mustard greens). These rotis were a major attraction and the kitchen seemed to produce a limitless supply.

Winter brought with it a variety of parathas, possibly a nostalgic remnant of my father's Punjabi ancestry. The stuffed paratha ruled – traditional ones with aloo (potato), gobi–matar (cauliflower–peas), or mooli (white radish), as well as parathas with winter greens mixed in the flour. Our cook's paneer parathas, made with fresh, home-made paneer kneaded into the dough with spices, tempted many friends to invite themselves over for a meal. While he loved a nice hot paratha, Bapu was a great advocate of a cold paratha (only one and made in pure ghee) and a bowl of any seasonal vegetables lightly sautéed with cumin, turmeric, and salt. This, he maintained, was the most balanced diet for lunch, "particularly in hot summer months".

As winter slowly turned to spring, Holi, the festival of colours, celebrated its arrival. The big, open courtyard where we ate winter lunch turned into a jamboree of people who were aunts and uncles of other people, nieces and nephews of other aunts and uncles, our parents' friends and their friends, and our friends and friends of those friends. My mother oversaw the kitchen and I think she enjoyed serving up a never-ending supply of food.

Samosas (fried pastries filled with spiced potatoes), gujias (sweet pastries) and, of course, the traditional bhang pakoras (fritters infused with cannabis leaves) started the day. Then, as the courtyard became a sea of coloured water with not a face recognizable, puri-aloo would start arriving.

When the heat of summer crept up, roti and rice became the preferred staples. I remember sooji (semolina) roti with a little ghee being a particular favourite. It was served with tori-aloo (sponge gourd and potato curry), which made a perfect summer combination. Fruit replaced sweet desserts, with dozens of varieties of mangoes making the summer more tolerable. Aam ki launj (sweet and tangy mango chutney), aam panna (a drink made from raw mangoes), and my favourite, a slice of mango with a hot roti were especially cherished.

My paternal grandfather introduced me to this simple pleasure – he would roll a long sliver of ripe mango in a hot roti, spread a good amount of ghee, and eat it with a knife and fork – he often ate his rotis like that. I did not have much patience for the knife and fork, so I just ate it like a kathi roll (a wrap made with paratha, filled with a variety of ingredients). I still haven't understood why this absolutely delicious preparation doesn't find a place on any chef's table.

The monsoon brought relief from the intense summer heat, along with the heady fragrance of wet earth and fresh vegetation. Fried food sounded appealing again and puris were especially tempting – stuffed puris, such as bedmis, puris made with seasonal flours, or even simple atta and maida puris. They were eaten with classic pairings such as aloo ki sabzi (potato curry) or kaddu ki sabzi (pumpkin curry). No one could resist the combination of eating puri with hot halwa (a sweet dish). It was the season when a variety of cooked chutneys such as tomato, kamrak ki launj (starfruit chutney), and karonde ki launj (Bengal currant chutney) found their way to the table.

A bonfire night in the winter of 1978 (left) and the family enjoying lunch out in the sun during a quintessential get-together, 1969 (right)

Cold puris also have their own unique place in my scrapbook of nostalgia. They had a very important place in train travel. Even today, an old-fashioned tiffin box remains amazingly evocative – of journeys with family, of puris, sukha aloo (dry potatoes), and achar (pickle) shared over 12 to 24 hours as the train click-clacked its way to our destination. Another one of my favourite memories is of waking up early to drive to the railway station with my mother, even when we did not have a train to catch. We went to enjoy the hot puri-aloo that vendors cooked fresh at the station for early morning passengers. These puris always tasted extra special for some reason – it may have been the touch of adventure or the thrill of enjoying them amid the bustling chaos of a railway platform.

Bhaturas were the other fried speciality that we went out to eat. While puris and parathas were regularly made at home, bhaturas never were. The whole family would pile into the car and drive out to Bengali Market near Connaught Place in New Delhi. This was the place to enjoy street food, especially puffed up bhaturas served with a side of chhole (chickpea curry). Each bowl of chhole had one large piece of potato stuck in it and was garnished with chopped ginger and fresh coriander. What I did not understand then, and still do not understand, is why bhaturas are served in pairs – though I must say I have no complaint with the addition at all.

Then the monsoon clouds made their way westward into the horizon, leaving behind the anticipation of the festival season. Dusshera, which commemorates the triumph of Lord Rama over Ravana, is preceded by nine days of fasting and feasting – fasting because only certain foods could be consumed and feasting because the alternative, fasting foods, the sweets, and the fruit, make up an entire cuisine category by itself. Each family has its own traditional specialities that have been fine-tuned over generations, and each one is exceptional.

On the tenth day the kitchen would go into overdrive. More than 30 people would crowd around the table for the lunch. With food restrictions lifted, the table groaned under the weight of celebratory puris, aloo ki sabzi, kaddu ki sabzi, seasonal vegetables, raita (a yoghurt-based condiment), halwa, and other sweets.

As this was the first big meal for those who had been fasting, a certain amount of bingeing was expected.

Twenty days later comes Diwali, the festival of lights. The days were filled with visits to family and friends, card parties brightened the evenings, and it seemed the kitchen never shut down. Diwali brought with it the first nip in the air, announcing that winter was on its way.

THE WARMTH OF THE FIRE

The passing of time marked by the seasons was measured by the food we ate and shared. As I grew in age and experience, exposure to cultures and cuisines across India seemed to underline this reality. Wherever I went, I found the roti – not always a staple made of wheat as I was familiar with in North India, but made with other grains, even lentils, depending on what was grown locally. I was intrigued by the many variations I tasted.

Every region, and every home, rolled out rotis in different forms, with different grains and different methods of cooking, but in essence they were all the same – an expression of warmth and caring. The phrase *roti kha kar jana* was all about hospitality, straight from the heart, genuine, with no formality about it at all. I experienced it regardless of which part of the country I was in, an extension of another phrase often heard while growing up: *aap hi ka ghar hai* or this is your home.

Over the years, closed doors have become the norm as noisy, gracious homes started giving way to silent, reserved flats and apartments, and joint families to nuclear families. Technology has galloped at an unstoppable pace and the world has shrunk even further. World cuisines, fine dining, and fast food have come to be preferred over home-cooked food. This is not necessarily a bad thing: what I regret is the loss of individual flavours that our mothers and grandmothers imbued their food with, the loss of that heritage. I regret the reduction in the size of dining tables that leaves no place for guests. I regret the loss of a culture of hospitality at home. *Roti kha kar jana* just does not seem relevant any longer.

This book is my tribute to those times and an attempt to bridge the chasm by handing down a collection of recipes – just roti recipes. Those that I grew up with, as well as those that were so affectionately shared. It is an attempt to ensure that cooking at home and recipes that emerged and complemented it are not lost.

This compilation is not exhaustive – it could never be. All I hope is that it will bring friends together and will revive traditions lost over time. That it will inspire experimentation at home by generations to come, as well as by all those who have enjoyed a variety of Indian rotis and would like to try making them for themselves.

The leisurely warmth, bonhomie, and conviviality that blossoms around the dining table at home cannot be replicated. You can order in rotis but a reheated roti just does not taste the same. The best rotis are made and served hot from the home kitchen.

Types of flour

A variety of grains and lentils are grown across the vast expanse of India. Many of these are ground into flour and used to make rotis. While mechanical mills and commercial flour production have rendered the traditional *chakki* (hand-rotated grinding stones) almost obsolete, they can still be seen in some rural areas.

The word "atta" refers to flour, specifically whole wheat flour in northern India. It is ideal for making rotis due to its balanced bran content, which makes it easy to knead and handle. For flours made from other grains or lentils, specific names are used in combination with the term "atta". These flours are often more coarsely ground and many are gluten-free. Since gluten-free flours can make the dough difficult to handle, a small amount of whole wheat flour or a binding agent, such as potato, may sometimes be added to improve its pliability.

Maida, or finely ground white flour, is highly refined and contains almost no bran. It is used to make deep-fried luchis (*see p162*), along with naans (*see p126*) and kulchas (*see p120*), which are popular fermented breads in India. Sooji, or semolina flour, made from durum wheat, when mixed with a small proportion of atta, also results in flavourful rotis. Bajre ka atta, or pearl millet flour, is predominantly produced in Rajasthan and enjoyed across northern India. Mixing a small amount of wheat flour with it helps to tone down its natural, slightly tart, flavour. Ragi atta, or finger millet flour, is traditionally used in southern and eastern India. Jowar atta, or sorghum flour, once a staple in Karnataka, is now primarily used for special occasions and festivals.

Makki atta, or maize flour, is a winter flour popular in northern India. Besan, or gram flour, is common throughout the country. When combined with other flours, its versatile nature can give an interesting range of rotis and parathas. Kuttu atta, or buckwheat flour, is found in northern and eastern India and, like the seasonal fibre-rich singhare ka atta, or water-chestnut flour, is mostly eaten during traditional Hindu fasting periods when the consumption of grain is prohibited.

Other flours, such as chana dal atta, or split chickpea flour, moong chilka atta, or split green gram flour, and poha, or flattened rice flour, are used to produce a range of interesting breads. However, these are not stand-alone flours as they really cannot be kneaded to form a pliable dough.

Kitchen tools

Implements for making rotis are quite different from the usual kitchen tools. Not only is it important to have these at hand for the texture and taste of the finished product, but also because the process of roasting and frying requires quick and dexterous handling, which is made easier and safer with the correct tools.

Tava Used for roasting bread, the traditional ones are heavy and made of iron, and can retain a more stable temperature. Today, terracotta and non-stick tavas are also popular.

Parat The traditional vessel in which dough is kneaded. It is flat and wide with raised sides to prevent spillage.

Jhaara/poni A perforated spoon with a long handle used for deep frying.

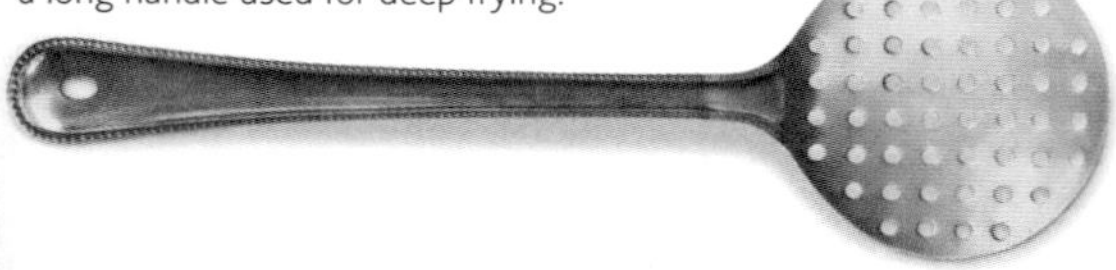

Palta A broad, flat, long-handled tool resembling a spatula, used to flip rotis and parathas on a hot tava.

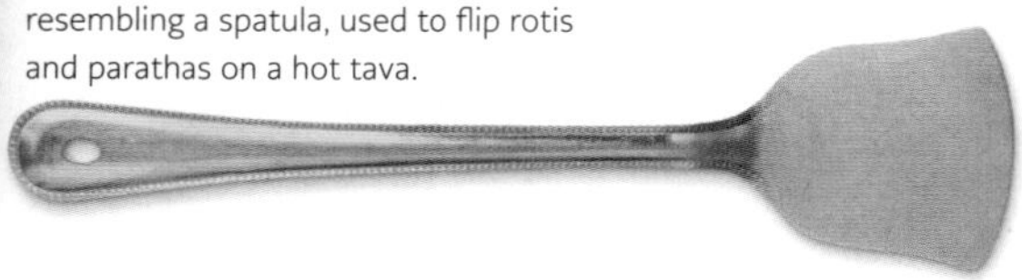

Chimta Straight tongs used to hold rotis over a direct flame to help them puff up.

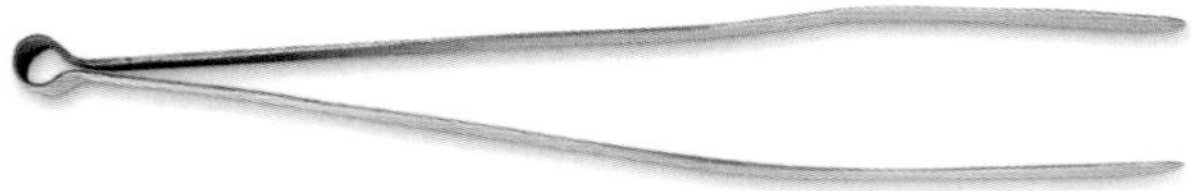

Kadhai A must in Indian kitchens, this is a heavy metal wok with a slightly broad base, designed specifically for deep frying.

Belan Rolling pin, which is almost always made of wood.

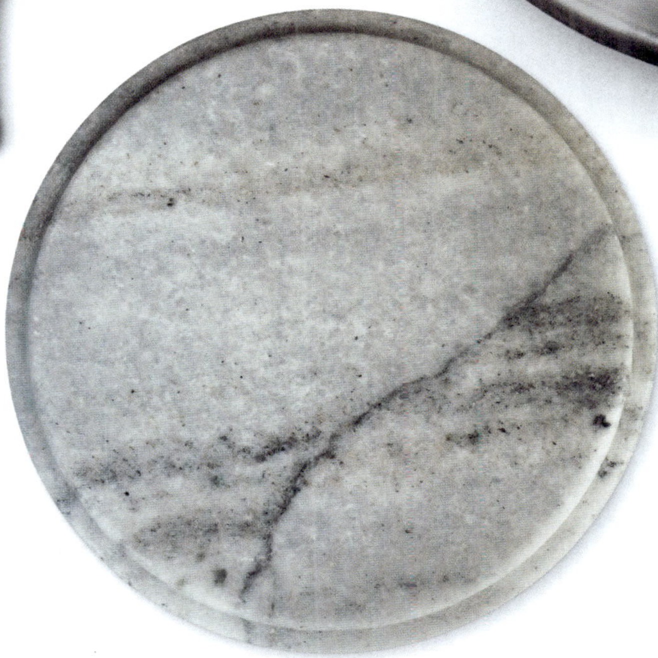

Chakla A flat circular slab of stone or wood on which rotis are rolled out.

Accompaniments

Accompaniments and traditional pairings, some of which are timeless, are an integral part of Indian meals. Their ingredients are seasonal, fresh, and often used raw to retain the maximum natural food value.

RAITAS

In India, raitas are yoghurt-based savoury dishes made with vegetables or a variety of greens, quite different from the sweet, fruit-flavoured yoghurts found in Western cuisine. Although some raitas are commonly paired with tandoori breads and meats – to complement the spicy main dishes with their cooling effect – there are no strict rules. For the best results, use fresh, high-quality vegetables and thick, well-set yoghurt. In Indian kitchens, roasted and ground cumin seeds are the most popular spice for flavouring raitas, with minced fresh coriander and green chilies adding the final touch.

Experimenting with and adjusting the flavours in any raita recipe is certainly possible. However, aloo paratha served with aloo raita might be less appealing unless you are a true aloo enthusiast. Vegetables such as cucumber and onion release water, especially after salt is added to them. To avoid a watery raita, add the salt just before serving. Raitas can be stored in the refrigerator for about two days, except when they contain onions. Onion-based raitas should always be made and eaten fresh, as raw onions can develop an unpleasant odour over time, which affects the taste of the raita.

CHUTNEYS

Chutneys are quick, spicy, and flavourful sauces that can complement almost any meal. While the recipes provided in this book are quite traditional, with a little imagination, a chutney can be conjured up from any number of everyday ingredients in the kitchen. Regional variations mean there is no one-size-fits-all rule, but chutneys typically align with seasonal ingredients – cooling coriander and mint chutneys for summer and spicier onion and garlic ones for winter.

It is important to note that chutneys are usually ground without adding water, which can dilute the flavour. The natural juices of the ingredients provide sufficient liquid content to allow grinding. Since most chutneys are uncooked, it is best to make small amounts to ensure they are consumed quickly – about two days in the refrigerator is the maximum they should be kept. Additionally, if raw onions are used, the chutney should not be stored at all.

ACHAR

In India, pickling means much more than merely extending the shelf life of food. Just like other accompaniments, they were developed predominantly to balance the digestive juices, thereby aiding digestion. Broadly, there are two traditional methods of pickling. The first one involves using oil, usually mustard and sesame oil. Pickles made in this way can be kept for up to a year. These oil-based pickles are prepared in two different ways. One way is to thoroughly coat the raw vegetables with salt and spices, place them in a ceramic or glass jar filled with oil, and leave to ferment in the sun. It may take anywhere from one to two weeks for this kind of pickle to be ready to eat. However, it has a fairly long shelf life if kept in the fridge. The other is to cook the vegetables in oil. Cooking results in a pickle that is ready to eat sooner but cannot be kept for too long.

The second method of pickling is more common in northern India for fresh winter vegetables such as carrots, cauliflower, turnips, radish, and beetroot. The vegetables are immersed in a water-based solution of ground yellow mustard seeds, chillies, and salt, and then fermented in the sun. Once ready to eat, these pickles should be consumed within a week or two. Pickling in brine and vinegar, though now increasingly popular, was not a method traditionally used in India.

Northern India has another type of quick and simple pickle that is frequently prepared in the hot summer months. All that is needed is lemon juice and salt, in which ingredients such as freshly grated ginger, slices of lemon, and green chillies are immersed and left to ferment for a couple of days. Once ready, the pickle can be refrigerated for up to a week.

It must be said that there are some pairings in Indian cuisine no amount of fusion or innovation has been able to change. Typical examples are chana-bhatura (*see pp176–179*), matra-kulcha (*see pp120–123*), sarson ka saag-makki ki roti (*see pp46–47*), dal-baati-churma (*see pp132–135*), and aloo-puri (*see pp158–161*). These traditional combinations, reiterated by the tastebuds of generation after generation, are now iconic – and that is how they are presented in this book.

DIY: White butter

Unsalted butter made by churning fresh cream

Ferment double cream in a covered bowl for 2 days until the cream begins to release water. Then use either a hand churner or electric whisk to churn the cream briskly until fat separates from the buttermilk as butter.

If needed, add 280ml (9½fl oz) cold water or 8–10 ice cubes to help the butter solidify.

Gently transfer to a small bowl and store in the refrigerator.

DIY: Ghee

Indian clarified butter

Make white butter from 1 litre (1¾ pints) of double cream.

Place the butter in a heavy-based pan and simmer on low heat until all the water evaporates.

Ghee clarifies into a clear, pale, golden liquid, leaving small granules that settle at the bottom of the pan. Take care not to let these granules char, as that will ruin the ghee.

DIY: Yoghurt

A dairy product obtained by coagulating milk

Warm 1 litre (1¾ pints) of milk (full-cream milk is preferable) in a heavy-based pan, but do not bring it to a boil.

Spread 45g (1½oz) of yoghurt culture on the sides and bottom of a terracotta pot. A ceramic, glass, or steel bowl can also be used. Pour in the warm milk and stir for 1 minute.

Cover and set aside for 6 hours or until the yoghurt is well-formed. Slight warmth helps the yoghurt set faster and better. On cold days, the milk should be slightly warmer and the bowl can be placed in a sunny spot or wrapped to retain heat as long as possible. Note that too much warmth will make the yoghurt sour.

DIY: Paneer

Fresh, Indian soft cheese made from curdled milk

Bring 1 litre (1¾ pints) full-cream milk to a boil in a pan, then stir in 45ml (1½fl oz) double cream, and bring to a boil again. Add 45ml (1½fl oz) yoghurt and stir until the milk curdles and the water separates from the casein. If this does not happen, add the juice of a medium-sized lemon. When the milk has curdled fully, strain in a colander lined with muslin or cheesecloth.

Fold the cloth to compress the paneer into a cube. Place this under a light weight, about 1kg (2¼lb), for 30 minutes to further compact it.

Unwrap and slice to use.

ROAST ON TAVA

Introduction

Eating a hot roti with butter or ghee is an almost sublime experience. It would be difficult to find anyone who disagrees with this statement. But, is there a standard, "typical" roti? The answer, quite obviously, is no. The roti is a non-fermented traditional Indian bread and, in a country as vast as India, every state, every town, every village, every household, in fact, has its own version of it. There can be many reasons for the difference – the type of flour used, or how much water is added to the dough, how long it is kneaded, how long it is left to breathe, is it rolled or patted out by hand, how thick or thin it is rolled out, is it finished on the tava or on the flame and, last but not the least, how much love has gone into its making.

Whole wheat flour is best for making an aromatic and tasty roti the Indian way, though flour from different sources may differ in taste and texture. Whole wheat flour is easily available in India, but if you cannot find it, look for a flour that is not highly refined, as those make a dough that is sticky and pasty. On the other hand, the flour should not have a high bran content either, as it does not allow the dough to bind well, which results in a roti that cracks easily.

Simple as it may be, water is essential to bind the dough. It may be necessary to make slight adjustments to the quantity given in recipes while kneading. Never pour in the water all at once – begin with a little and mix it in the flour, add some more and collect all the flour into one crumbly whole. Start kneading, adding a little water at a time as you go along till you have one compact dough ball that does not fall apart. It should not be too stiff or hard – if you think it is, sprinkle a little more water. A good roti dough is soft and pliable.

After kneading, the dough must be kept aside for a minimum of 15 minutes. This allows the gluten to develop properly, increasing the overall elasticity of the dough, making it easier to roll out and resulting in softer rotis. It is important to cover the dough when it is kept aside to prevent a crust forming on the surface as it dries out. This dry, grainy crust will hinder the smooth rolling of the roti and may cause it to tear.

Making dough balls is not just about portioning the dough. A perfect disc will make it easier to achieve a circular roti.

Making dough balls for individual rotis is not merely about portioning the dough. The dough should be shaped into perfect spheres by applying gentle pressure as they are rolled between the palms, and then flattened to a disc. A perfect disc will make it easier to achieve a circular roti. From here, there are two basic ways to extend the disc to the required size. One is to use a rolling pin – it is awe-inspiring to watch the proficient lightly wield a rolling pin as the dough disc, seemingly of its own volition, rotates slowly under it to extend into a perfect circle. As a beginner, it is fine to lift and turn the dough while rolling out the rotis to achieve the circular shape. While dry flour is needed to prevent the dough sticking to the work surface, keep in mind the amount of dry flour used makes a difference – too much tends to dry out the roti.

The other way to make a roti is to not use a rolling pin at all. Instead, flatten and extend the dough ball by pressing it between your palms. This is a common method in homes where slightly thicker rotis are preferred. These handcrafted rotis are just as delicious, though there is a slight difference in the final texture as a rolling pin presses and packs the dough more tightly. The hand technique is also preferred for flours from other grains that are difficult to handle.

Rotis are best cooked on a tava. Always warm the tava on medium heat before placing the roti on it. A slight colour change signals that it is time to flip the roti. Having flipped it, watch for tiny blisters that form on the surface. Flip again if they do not form, as these indicate that the roti is ready to face the flame. Remove the tava, turn up the flame, place the roti directly on it, and let it puff up.

While rotis are best served hot, modern lifestyles are not always conducive to such luxury. If not serving immediately, what works best is to spread some ghee – as much or as little as you are comfortable with – evenly between two rotis by rubbing them together. Then place the paired rotis in a double-walled insulated container with a paper napkin lining the base. When the rotis have cooled a bit, cover them with another paper napkin and close the box. The paper napkins will absorb any moisture, preventing the rotis from getting soggy and they will remain soft.

Rotis can also be stored in the refrigerator for about two days. They must be cooled, then kept in an airtight container, or wrapped in cling-film or foil. Reheat them on a tava on medium heat. If using a microwave, place them between two paper napkins in a covered dish for 30 seconds.

While whole wheat flour is the primary flour used for rotis, one cannot overlook the large variety of rotis made of other grains eaten all over the country. Regional differences in the grains used were based on seasonal availability. Today, with modern storage facilities and transportation, "seasonal" is no longer relevant. However, fresh, in-season flours are the best flours to use as they are without preservatives. If buying packaged flours, which are more easily available, it is important to check the production and use-by dates.

Over the years, experimentation and a desire for variation have given rise to two offshoots of the simple roti. One, by adding ingredients to the dough – dry spices, including salt, and minced fresh herbs. These can be added directly to the flour and dry-mixed before kneading. Wet ingredients such

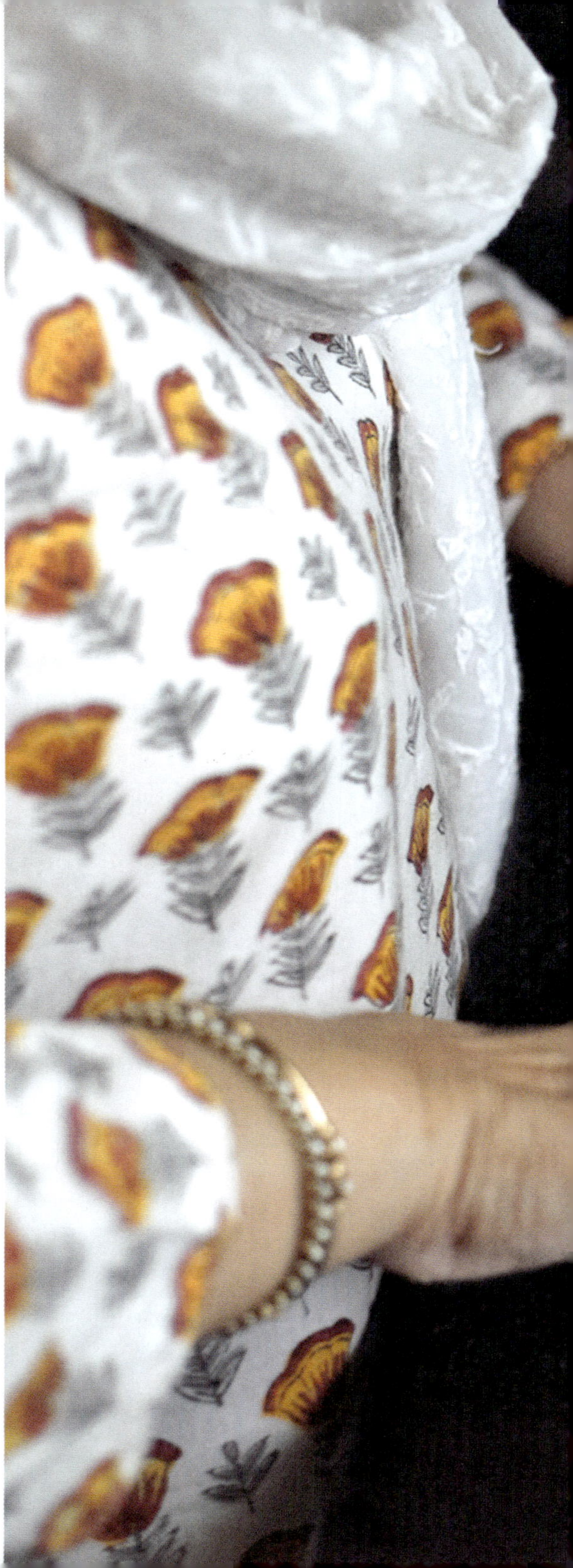

as leafy greens and cooked lentils can also be added. These actually serve as the binder, in which case very little or almost no water is required while kneading. Ingredients such as fresh, non-set paneer can also be crumbled into the dry flour and then kneaded while sprinkling water to make the dough. The one exception I have found is that fresh tomatoes cannot be added to the dough – they can be used only if cooked till all their water content is lost.

The second is the art of making a stuffed roti, which is specific to every household. To my mind, stuffed rotis may have started off as a "no waste" preference. Any leftover cooked vegetables can be mashed and stuffed into a roti. The addition of minced fresh coriander before mashing the leftover vegetables gives a fresh flavour to these rotis. But, whether leftover or fresh, it is important that the stuffing be dry and at room temperature. If it is warm or there is even a hint of water, the dough will not roll out. This is also why stuffed rotis are almost always made from whole wheat flour – the dough is pliable and lends itself to being stretched and pulled as required.

The following pages also give recipes for different types of rotis from all over the country. Many use flours of other grains that are often difficult to knead and roll. While some of these are combined with wheat flour to promote elasticity and assist in binding, in others a binding agent may be used. Individual recipes for these seasonal and traditional rotis indicate how to handle them.

While a roti may look simple, its making is anything but – do not get disheartened if your first attempt, the second, or even the third looks nothing like it should. The secret is that practice makes perfect!

Phulka or Chapati

Everyone's favourite "roti" – a basic, flat, unleavened bread

Makes 6
Prep 40 minutes
Cook 15–20 minutes

280g (9¾oz) atta (whole wheat flour)
15ml (½fl oz) ghee or 15g (½oz) butter, for brushing

Set aside 35g (1¼oz) of atta in a platter and place the remaining atta in a deep bowl. Slowly add 105ml (3½fl oz) of water, while kneading the atta into a pliable dough that does not stick to your hand or the bowl. Cover with a thin muslin cloth and keep for 30 minutes.

Divide the dough into 6 equal portions and keep them covered while rolling the rotis so the dough does not dry out. Take one portion and roll into a smooth ball between your palms. Flatten the ball, turn over in the platter of atta and, using a rolling pin, roll out evenly to about 20cm (8in) in diameter.

Place a tava on medium heat and wait till it warms before transferring the rolled-out dough onto it. Turn over once or twice to roast both sides evenly. Take the tava off the heat and use a pair of tongs to place the roti on the direct flame to puff it up. Remove quickly before it chars.

Alternatively, rotis can also be puffed up on the tava. After both sides are roasted, turn the heat to low. Wear an oven glove and firmly, but gently, press down with your fingers while rotating the roti on the tava until it puffs up.

Brush with ghee or butter and serve hot.

Perfect when puffed up like a ball.

Sindhi roti

From Sindh, a softer, richer version

Makes 6
Prep 40 minutes
Cook 20–25 minutes

280g (9¾oz) atta (whole wheat flour)
60ml (2fl oz) ghee

Reserve 35g (1¼oz) atta in a platter and place the rest in a deep bowl. Knead a pliable dough that does not stick to your hand or the bowl by adding about 105ml (3½fl oz) of water in stages as required. Cover with a thin muslin cloth and keep for 30 minutes.

Divide the dough into 6 equal portions. Keep these covered while rolling the rotis so that the dough does not dry out. Shape one portion into a smooth ball between your palms. Flatten it gently, turn over in the platter of atta, and roll out evenly to about 20cm (8in) in diameter.

Place a tava on medium heat and wait till it warms. Then, place the rolled-out dough on it and turn over once or twice to roast both sides evenly. Reduce the heat and spread about 1 tsp ghee on the roti. Fold it into half and spread about ¼ tsp ghee on it. Fold again into a quarter and spread about ¼ tsp ghee on the surface. Flip the roti and apply gentle pressure while spreading about ¼ tsp ghee on this side as well. Remove from tava and serve hot.

These rotis can be made earlier and kept in a warm box – they will remain soft.

Perfect when the roti has absorbed the ghee.

Do palli roti

Soft, light, almost paper-thin rotis, a treat for guests

Makes 12
Prep 1 hour 10 minutes
Cook 20–25 minutes

280g (9¾oz) atta (whole wheat flour)
245g (8½oz) maida (all-purpose flour)
1 tsp salt
30ml (1fl oz) vegetable oil
30ml (1fl oz) ghee

Having set aside 35g (1¼oz) of atta in a platter, place the remaining flours, salt, and oil in a deep bowl and mix well. Slowly add about 105ml (3½fl oz) of water, while kneading the flours into a pliable, non-sticky dough. Cover with a damp cloth and keep for 1 hour.

Divide the dough into 12 equal portions. Cover with a thin muslin cloth while rolling the rotis, so the dough does not dry out. Take one portion and shape into a smooth ball between your palms. Flatten, turn over in the platter of atta, and roll out evenly to about 15cm (6in) in diameter. Repeat with another portion.

Spread ½ tsp ghee on one rolled-out roti, sprinkle with a little atta, and cover with the second rolled-out roti. Now roll out the twin rotis to about 20–23cm (8–9in) in diameter.

Place a tava on medium heat. Once it is warm, transfer the twin rotis onto it. Turn over once or twice to roast both sides evenly. Remove from tava, gently separate the rotis, and serve hot.

Perfect when the twin rotis can be easily separated.

Bhakri

A savoury breakfast bread from Gujarat and Maharashtra

Makes 6
Prep 40 minutes
Cook 20–25 minutes

420g (14¼oz) atta (whole wheat flour)
1½ tsp salt
10g (¼oz) cumin seeds, roasted and ground
45g (1½oz) fresh coriander, minced
45ml (1½fl oz) ghee

Set aside 35g (1¼oz) of atta in a platter. Place the remaining atta in a deep bowl, add salt, cumin seeds, and fresh coriander, and mix well. Then crumble the ghee into the atta. Slowly add about 140ml (4¾fl oz) of water, while kneading atta into a pliable dough that does not stick to your hand or the bowl. Cover with a thin muslin cloth and keep for 30 minutes.

Divide the dough into 6 equal portions and keep covered while rolling the rotis, so the dough does not dry out. Take one portion and roll into a smooth ball between your palms. Flatten the ball, turn over in the platter of atta, and, using a rolling pin, roll out evenly till about 15–17cm (6–7in) in diameter. Bhakri is slightly thick. Prick the surface lightly with a fork in 2–3 places.

Place a tava on medium heat and wait till it warms before transferring the rolled-out dough onto it. Allow the bhakri to get slightly roasted on both sides. Put on an oven glove and, firmly but gently press down with your fingers while rotating the bhakri on the tava so that it roasts thoroughly. Turn over once or twice to roast both sides evenly. Repeat the process till all the bhakris are ready.

Perfect when cooked to a pale golden-brown.

Khamiri roti

A light, spongy, slightly tart bread from the Mughal era

Makes 6
Prep 40 minutes
Rest 6–7 hours
Cook 20–25 minutes

280g (9¾oz) atta (whole wheat flour)
1 tsp salt
1 tsp red chilli powder
1 tsp carom seeds
15ml (½fl oz) ghee or 15g (½oz) butter, for brushing

Set aside 35g (1¼oz) of atta in a platter. Place the remaining atta and all the other ingredients in a deep bowl and mix well. Slowly add about 105ml (3½fl oz) of water while kneading the atta into a pliable dough that does not stick to your hand or the bowl. Cover with a thin muslin cloth and keep for 6–7 hours so that it ferments naturally, then knead again.

Divide the dough into 6 equal portions. Make sure these remain covered while rolling the rotis so the dough does not dry out. Take one portion and roll into a smooth ball between your palms. Flatten the ball, turn over in the platter of atta and, using a rolling pin, roll out evenly to about 20cm (8in) in diameter.

Place a tava on medium heat and wait till it warms before transferring the rolled-out dough onto it. Turn over once or twice to roast both sides evenly. Take the tava off the heat and use a pair of tongs to place the roti on the direct heat to puff it up. Remove quickly before it chars. Brush with ghee or butter and serve hot.

Perfect when fluffy, soft, and chewy.

Ragi roti

Typical of the southern states, such as Karnataka and Andhra Pradesh

Makes 6
Prep 15 minutes
Cook 20–25 minutes

105g (3¾oz) atta (whole wheat flour)
210g (7½oz) ragi atta (finger millet flour)
30g (1oz) fresh coriander, minced
1 tsp salt
1 green chilli, minced (optional)
30ml (1fl oz) vegetable oil
35g (1¼oz) onion paste
15ml (½fl oz) ghee or 15g (½oz) butter, for brushing

Set aside about 35g (1¼oz) of atta in a platter and place the remaining flours in a deep bowl. Mix in the fresh coriander, salt, and green chilli (if using). Add the oil and onion paste and mix well. Boil 105ml (3½fl oz) of water, pour over the flours, and stir in gently with a spoon. When the mix has cooled just enough to be handled (before it becomes cold), knead to a soft and pliable dough that does not stick to your hand or the bowl. Sprinkle a little more water, only if needed, to soften the dough.

Divide the dough into 6 equal portions. Remember to cover with a thin muslin cloth while rolling the rotis, so that the dough does not dry out. Shape one portion into a smooth ball between your palms. Flatten, turn over in the platter of atta, and roll out evenly to about 15–17cm (6–7in) in diameter.

Place a tava on medium heat and wait till it warms before placing the rolled-out dough onto it. Keep the heat low to medium as this is a thick roti that needs time to cook. Turn over once or twice to roast both sides evenly. Brush with butter or ghee and serve hot. Repeat the process till all the rotis are ready.

Perfect when brown and slightly crispy.

Lesu or Mandua ki roti

An interesting synergy of textures from Uttarakhand

Makes 6
Prep 25–30 minutes
Cook 20–25 minutes

350g (12¼oz) atta (whole wheat flour)
1½ tsp salt
210g (7½oz) ragi atta (finger millet flour)
1 tsp carom seeds
1 tsp red chilli powder
30g (1oz) fresh coriander, minced
30ml (1fl oz) vegetable oil
15ml (½fl oz) ghee or 15g (½oz) butter, for brushing

Reserve about 35g (1¼oz) of atta in a platter, place the remaining atta in a deep bowl, add salt, and mix well. Slowly add 105ml (3½fl oz) of water and make a pliable dough that does not stick to your hands or the bowl. Cover with a thin muslin cloth and keep for 30 minutes.

Place the ragi atta in a deep bowl with the remaining ingredients. Bring 105ml (3½fl oz) of water to boil, pour over the flour, and stir in gently with a spoon. Wait till the mix cools just enough to be handled (it should not become cold) and knead to a soft and pliable dough. Divide the dough into 6 equal portions. Keep covered while rolling the rotis, so the dough does not dry out.

Take one portion of whole wheat dough and roll into a smooth ball between your palms. Flatten to about 10cm (4in) in diameter with your fingers. Place one portion of ragi dough in the centre of the flattened dough, lift the edges to make a pouch, enclose, and seal the ball of ragi in it. Flatten the pouch, turn over in a platter of atta and, using a rolling pin, roll out evenly to about 15–17cm (6–7in) in diameter.

Place a tava on medium heat and wait till it warms before transferring the rolled-out dough onto it. Turn over and roast both sides evenly, till well done. Brush with butter or ghee and eat hot.

Perfect when the ragi filling comes as a surprise.

Makki ki roti, with sarson ka saag

A winter favourite from Punjab

Makes 6
Prep 10 minutes
Cook 15–20 minutes

245g (8½oz) makki atta
70g (2¼oz) atta (whole wheat flour)
1 tsp salt
1 tsp red chilli powder
75ml (2½fl oz) ghee

FOR SARSON KA SAAG

280g (9¾oz) sarson (mustard greens)
140g (5oz) palak (spinach leaves)
70g (2¼oz) bathua (goosefoot greens)
35g (1¼oz) methi (fenugreek greens)
35g (1¼oz) fresh coriander
3–4 garlic cloves
70g (2¼oz) onion
2 whole red chillies
2 tsp salt
30g (1oz) besan (gram flour)

Mix both flours, salt, and red chilli powder in a deep bowl. Slowly add about 105ml (3½fl oz) of tepid water to make a pliable dough that does not stick to your hand or the bowl. Divide the dough into 6 equal portions. Cover with a damp muslin cloth and keep for 30 minutes.

Place a tava to warm on medium heat. Take one portion of dough and shape into a smooth ball between your palms. Flatten and pat in between with your palms to flatten further. Moisten your palms to keep the dough from sticking and continue patting till the roti is about 15cm (6in) in diameter, then gently place it on the warm tava. Turn over a few times until the colour lightens and small golden-brown patches show on the surface. Spread ghee or butter and keep roasting for another minute. Remove from tava. The makki ki roti should be chewy with a light brown edge

To make the saag, remove any thick stems from the sarson and palak, and soak all the greens for 15 minutes. Drain, wash in cold water, then place in a pressure cooker. Add all other saag ingredients except the gram flour. Pour in 280ml (9¾fl oz) of water, close the lid, and bring to full pressure on medium heat. Then reduce the heat and cook for another 15 minutes. Set aside to cool.

For tempering

30ml (1fl oz) ghee

½ tsp asafoetida powder

1 whole red chilli

1 tsp garlic, minced

1 tsp ginger, minced

35g (1¼oz) butter

Remove the greens from the pressure cooker and mash or blend in a mixer-grinder till smooth. Place back in the pressure cooker pan, add the cornmeal and 15g (½oz) of ghee and cook on medium heat for 7–10 minutes without closing the lid. Stir every now and then so that the saag does not stick to the bottom.

Heat the ghee for tempering in a small pan, add the asafoetida powder and whole red chilli. Stir and add the ginger and garlic. Roast till well done and smoky, then add to the saag. Simmer for a minute or two.

Add a dollop of butter and serve hot with the makki ki roti.

Jolada rotti

Sorghum-based roti from Karnataka

Makes 6
Prep 15 minutes
Cook 20–25 minutes

- 70g (2¼oz) atta (whole wheat flour)
- 280g (9¾oz) jowar atta (sorghum flour)
- 1 tsp black pepper, coarsely ground
- 1 tsp cumin, roasted and ground
- 1 tsp salt
- 15ml (½fl oz) ghee or 15g (½oz) butter, for brushing

Having set aside 35g (1¼oz) atta in a platter, in a deep bowl, mix the remaining flours, black pepper, cumin seeds, and salt. Bring 105ml (3½fl oz) of water to boil, pour over the flours, and stir in gently with a spoon. Wait till the mix cools just enough to be handled (it should not become cold), then knead a soft and pliable dough that does not stick to your hands or the bowl. If needed, sprinkle a little more water to soften the dough.

Divide the dough into 6 equal portions. Keep the dough covered with a thin muslin cloth while rolling the rotis, so that it does not dry out. Take one portion and shape a smooth ball between the palms of your hands. Flatten, turn over in the platter of atta, and roll out evenly to about 15–17cm (6–7in) in diameter.

Warm a tava on medium heat and transfer the rolled-out dough onto it. This roti is slightly thick, so keep the heat low to medium. Roast until the surface blisters, then flip gently to roast the other side. Wear an oven glove and, firmly but gently, press down with your fingers while rotating the roti on the tava so that it roasts thoroughly. Brush with ghee or butter and serve hot.

Perfect when light brown and slightly crispy.

Bajre ki roti

From the semi-arid regions of western India

Makes 6
Prep 25 minutes
Cook 15–20 minutes

210g (7½oz) bajra atta (pearl millet flour)
140g (5oz) atta (whole wheat flour)
1 tsp salt
15ml (½fl oz) ghee or 15g (½oz) butter, for brushing

Place both flours in a deep bowl, add the salt, and mix well. Slowly add about 105ml (3½fl oz) of tepid water to make a pliable dough that does not stick to your hand or the bowl. Cover with a thin muslin cloth and keep aside for 15 minutes, then knead lightly again.

Divide the dough into 6 equal portions. Make sure the dough is covered while rolling the rotis so that the dough does not dry out. Take one portion and roll into a smooth ball between your palms. Flatten the ball and pat between your palms to flatten further. Moisten your palms to keep the dough from sticking and continue patting till the roti is about 15cm (6in) in diameter.

Place a tava on medium heat and wait till it warms before transferring the rolled-out dough onto it. Turn over a few times until the colour lightens and small brown patches show on the surface. Spread ghee or butter and continue to roast for a minute.

Perfect when soft and chewy.

PAIR IT WITH

LEHSUN–PYAAZ CHUTNEY

Grind 140g (5oz) onions, 1 garlic clove, 1–2 red chillies, 1 tsp salt and 1 tsp lemon juice in a mixer-grinder without adding any water at all. If ground with a pestle and mortar, the result is an even more flavourful chutney.

Rumali roti

Thin to the point of being translucent like a rumaal – a handkerchief!

Makes 6
Prep 40 minutes
Cook 40 minutes

280g (9¾oz) atta (whole wheat flour)
140g (5oz) maida (all-purpose flour)
1 tsp salt

Set aside 35g (1¼oz) of atta in a platter. Place the remaining flours in a deep bowl, add salt, and mix well. Slowly add about 105ml (3½fl oz) of water, while kneading the flours into a pliable dough – this dough has to be a little sticky, so you may need a little more water. Cover with a damp cloth and keep for 30 minutes, then knead again for a couple of minutes.

Divide the dough into 6 equal portions. Cover with a thin muslin cloth while rolling the rotis so the dough does not dry out. Take one portion and roll into a smooth ball between your palms. Flatten the ball, turn over in the platter of atta, and, using a rolling pin, roll out evenly till about 25cm (10in) in diameter – these rotis are almost paper thin.

Place a kadhai or a tava upside down on medium heat and wait till it heats up. When a pinch of flour sprinkled on the inverted vessel turns golden, it has reached the right temperature; drape the rolled-out dough on it. Turn over once or twice to roast both sides evenly. Serve immediately, as these rotis do not store well.

Perfect when small, golden-brown blisters mark the surface.

Aloo ki roti

A classic, with a mouthwatering appeal for all ages

Makes 6
Prep 40 minutes
Cook 20–25 minutes

420g (14¼oz) atta (whole wheat flour)
15ml (½fl oz) ghee or 15g (½oz) butter, for brushing

For stuffing
250g (8¾oz) potatoes
45g (1½oz) fresh coriander, minced
1 tsp red chilli powder
10g (¼oz) cumin seeds, roasted and ground
1 tsp salt
2–3 green chillies, minced (optional)

PAIR IT WITH

DHANIA-PUDINA CHUTNEY

Grind 140g (5oz) fresh coriander, 15g (½oz) mint leaves, 35g (1¼oz) onions, 35g (1¼oz) tomatoes, 2 green chillies, and 1 tsp of salt in a mixer-grinder without adding any water at all. Add 2 tsp lemon juice, mix well, and serve.

Set aside 35g (1¼oz) of atta in a platter. Place the remaining atta in a deep bowl. Slowly add about 140ml (4¾fl oz) of water while kneading the atta into a pliable dough that does not stick to your hand or the bowl. Cover and keep for 30 minutes.

Boil, cool, and peel the potatoes, crumble coarsely, then add all the other ingredients for the stuffing and mash to a smooth consistency. Divide into 6 equal portions and set aside.

Divide the dough into 6 equal portions. Cover with a thin muslin cloth while rolling the rotis, so the dough does not dry out. Take one portion and roll into a smooth ball between your palms. Flatten the ball, turn over in the platter of atta and, using a rolling pin, roll out evenly to about 10cm (4in) in diameter. Place one portion of the stuffing in the centre of the roti, lift the edges to make a pouch, enclose the mix, and seal the dough pouch. Gently flatten the pouch, turn over in the platter of atta, and roll out, making sure to flip sides at least once. Use a little dry atta to cover any potato stuffing if exposed.

Warm a tava and place the stuffed roti on it. Roast, turning over once or twice. As soon as it becomes brown, remove, brush with ghee or butter, and serve hot.

Making rotis, especially stuffed rotis, can be daunting. To start, it may be better to make 2, almost full-size rotis. Spread the filling on one and cover it with the other. Press all around to seal the edges, roll gently with rolling pin, and roast.

Perfect when it cooks to a nice golden colour.

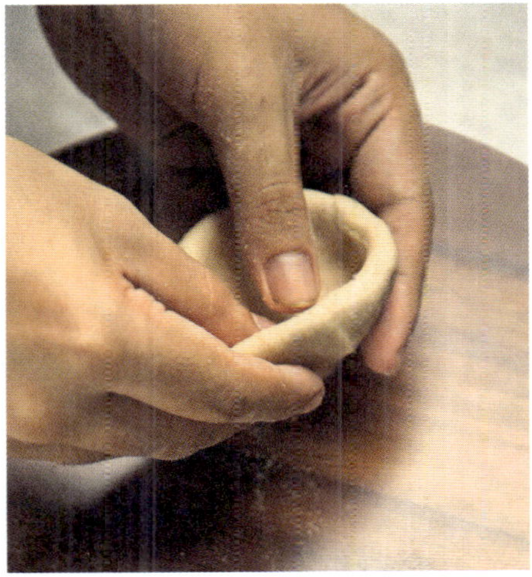

Matar bhari roti

Fresh, tender peas make for a zesty stuffing

Makes 6
Prep 1 hour
Cook 20–25 minutes

420g (14¼oz) atta (whole wheat flour)
15ml (½fl oz) ghee or 15g (½oz) butter, for brushing

For stuffing
280g (9½oz) peas, shelled
10g (¼oz) cumin seeds, roasted and ground
¼ tsp turmeric powder
½ tsp asafoetida powder
1 tsp red chilli powder
1 tsp ginger paste
30g (1oz) fresh coriander, minced
2–3 green chillies, minced
1½ tsp salt
1 tsp vegetable oil

Set aside 35g (1¼oz) of atta in a platter. Place the remaining atta in a deep bowl. Slowly add about 140ml (4¾fl oz) of water while kneading the atta into a pliable dough, which does not stick to your hand or the bowl. Cover and keep for 30 minutes.

To make the peas stuffing, in a heavy-based pan add all the ingredients and mix well. Add about 140ml (4¾fl oz) of water, cover, and cook on low heat – stirring once or twice till the peas are well cooked, and the water is completely absorbed. Remove from the heat, mash well to a smooth consistency. Divide into 6 equal portions and let it cool.

Divide the dough into 6 equal portions. Cover with a thin muslin cloth while rolling the rotis, so the dough does not dry out. Take one portion and roll into a smooth ball between your palms. Flatten the ball, turn over in the platter of atta and, using a rolling pin, roll out evenly to about 10cm (4in) in diameter. Place one portion of the stuffing in the centre of the roti, lift the edges to make a pouch, enclose the mix, and seal it. Gently flatten the pouch, turn over in the platter of atta, and roll out, making sure to flip sides at least once. Pat with dry atta to cover any exposed peas stuffing.

Warm a tava and place the stuffed roti on it. Roast, turning over once or twice. As soon as it browns, remove, brush with ghee or butter and serve hot.

Perfect when it cooks to a nice golden colour.

Gajar-Methi ki roti

An interesting variation of the stuffed roti with crunchy carrots and greens

Makes 6
Prep 1 hour
Cook 20–25 minutes

420g (14¼oz) atta (whole wheat flour)
15ml (½fl oz) ghee or 15g (½oz) butter, for brushing

For stuffing

1 tsp vegetable oil
1 tsp cumin seeds
¼ tsp turmeric powder
10g (¼oz) red chilli powder
35g (1¼oz) fenugreek leaves, finely chopped
280g (9¾oz) carrots, finely chopped
30g (1oz) fresh coriander, minced
1½ tsp salt

Set aside 35g (1¼oz) of atta in a platter. Place the remaining atta in a deep bowl. Slowly add about 140ml (4¾fl oz) of water while kneading the atta into a pliable dough, which does not stick to your hand or the bowl. Cover and keep for 30 minutes.

To make the carrot-fenugreek stuffing, heat the oil in a heavy-based pan. Add cumin seeds, turmeric, and chilli powder, stir for few seconds, then add the fenugreek leaves, stir, and add the carrots, fresh coriander, and salt. Cover and cook till the carrots are soft, and there is no liquid in the pan at all. Allow to cool, then mash to a smooth consistency. Divide into 6 equal portions and cool before using as stuffing for each roti.

Divide the dough into 6 equal portions. Cover with a thin muslin cloth while rolling the rotis, so the dough does not dry out. Take one portion and roll into a smooth ball between your palms. Flatten the ball, turn over in the platter of atta and, using a rolling pin, roll out evenly to about 10cm (4in) in diameter. Place one portion of the stuffing in the centre of the roti, lift the edges to make a pouch, enclose the mix, and seal it. Gently flatten the pouch, turn over in the platter of atta, and roll out, making sure to flip sides at least once. Pat with dry atta to cover any exposed stuffing.

Warm a tava and place the stuffed roti on it. Roast, turning over once or twice. As soon as it browns, remove, brush with ghee or butter and serve hot.

Perfect when the discrete flavours can be tasted.

Paneer roti

Soft, flavourful, and hearty – this is a classic

Makes 6
Prep 1 hour
Cook 20–25 minutes

420g (14¼oz) atta (whole wheat flour)
15ml (½fl oz) ghee or 15g (½oz) butter, for brushing

For stuffing
210g (7½oz) paneer
30g (1oz) fresh coriander, minced
10g (¼oz) red chilli powder
10g (¼oz) cumin seeds, roasted and ground
1½ tsp salt

PAIR IT WITH

AAM KI LAUNJ

Take 280g (9¾oz) raw mangoes, peel, deseed and cut like finger chips. Sprinkle 10g (¼oz) of salt, and set aside for 1 hour, then drain. Heat 10ml (¼fl oz) oil in a heavy-based pan and add 10g (¼oz) panch phoran masala (*see pp162–163*). When it splutters, add 2 whole red chillies, mango strips, ¼ tsp turmeric powder, and stir well. Add 70ml (2¼fl oz) of water, cover, and cook on medium heat till the mangoes are soft. Stir in 140g (5oz) sugar and cook till the mangoes take on a glazed appearance. Serve hot or cold.

Having set aside 35g (1¼oz) of atta in a platter, place the remaining atta in a deep bowl. Slowly add about 140ml (4¾fl oz) of water while kneading the atta into a pliable dough that does not stick to your hand or the bowl. Cover with a thin muslin cloth and keep for 30 minutes.

Place the paneer in a bowl, add the fresh coriander, chilli powder, cumin seeds, and salt, and mix til smooth. Divide into 6 equal portions.

Divide the dough into 6 equal portions. Remember to keep it covered while rolling the rotis so the dough does not dry out. Roll one portion into a smooth ball between your palms. Flatten the ball, turn over in a platter of dry atta, and roll out evenly to about 10cm (4in) in diameter.

Place a portion of the paneer mix in the centre and lift the edges of the atta to make a pouch to enclose it, and seal the edges. Press gently to flatten and roll out to about 18cm (7in) in diameter, turning on both sides and using a little dry atta to cover the paneer mix if it gets exposed.

Place a tava on medium heat and wait till it warms up before transferring the stuffed roti onto it. Turn over once or twice to roast both sides evenly. Remove from tava as soon as it browns and serve hot with ghee or butter. Repeat the process till all the rotis are ready.

Perfect when golden and crisp on the outside, soft on the inside.

Hari mirch and zeera roti

Spicy green chillies paired with cumin seeds add a delightful zing

Makes 6
Prep 50 minutes
Cook 15–20 minutes

35g (1¼oz) fresh coriander, minced
2–3 green chillies, minced
1 tsp cumin seeds
280g (9¾oz) atta (whole wheat flour)
1 tsp salt
1 tsp vegetable oil
15ml (½fl oz) ghee or 15g (½oz) butter, for brushing

PAIR IT WITH

ALOO KA RAITA

Take 140g (5oz) yoghurt. Whisk in 1 tsp each of roasted and ground cumin, red chilli powder, and salt. Add 35g (1¼oz) minced, fresh coriander and 140g (5oz) boiled, peeled, and diced potatoes. Mix well and serve cold.

Grind the fresh coriander, green chillies, and cumin seeds together in a dry grinder.

Set aside 35g (1¼oz) of atta in a platter. Place the remaining atta in a deep bowl, add the salt, the coriander-chilli paste, and mix. Crumble the oil into the atta. Slowly add about 105ml (3½fl oz) of water while kneading the atta into a pliable dough that does not stick to your hand or the bowl. Cover with a thin muslin cloth and keep aside for 30 minutes.

Divide the dough into 6 equal portions. Keep the dough covered while rolling the rotis so that it does not dry out. Take one portion and roll into a smooth ball between your palms. Flatten the ball, turn over in the platter of atta and, using a rolling pin, roll out evenly to about 20cm (8in) in diameter.

Place a tava on medium heat and wait till it warms before transferring the rolled-out dough onto it. Turn over once or twice to roast both sides evenly. After both sides are roasted, turn the heat to low, wear an oven glove, and gently, but firmly, press the roti with your fingers while rotating it on the tava. This will puff up the roti. Brush with ghee or butter and serve hot.

Perfect when puffed up like a ball.

Missi roti

Gram flour or besan brings a nutty flavour to this north Indian winter favourite

Makes 6
Prep 25 minutes
Rest 1 hour
Cook 20–25 minutes

- 140g (5oz) atta (whole wheat flour)
- 140g (5oz) besan (gram flour)
- 30g (1oz) fresh coriander, minced
- 30g (1oz) mint leaves, minced
- 1½ tsp black pepper, powdered
- 1 tsp cumin seeds, roasted and ground
- 1 tsp raw mango powder
- 1 tsp vegetable oil
- 1 tsp salt
- 15ml (½fl oz) ghee or 15g (½oz) butter, for brushing

PAIR IT WITH

KAMRAK KI LAUNJ

Heat 10ml (¼fl oz) vegetable oil in a heavy-based pan and add 10g (¼oz) of panch phoran masala (*see pp162–163*). When it splutters, add 2 whole red chillies, 280g (9¾oz) starfruit cut in cross section, ¼ tsp turmeric powder, 1 tsp red chilli powder, and 1½ tsp salt. Add 70ml (2¼fl oz) of water, cover, and cook on medium heat till the starfruit has reduced to half its quantity. Add 105g (3½oz) sugar and cook till the starfruit takes on a glazed appearance. Serve hot or cold.

Set aside 35g (1¼oz) of atta in a platter. Place the remaining atta in a deep bowl, add all the other ingredients, and mix. Slowly add about 105ml (3½fl oz) of water while kneading the flours into a pliable dough that does not stick to your hand or the bowl. Cover with a thin muslin cloth and keep for 1 hour.

Divide the dough into 6 equal portions and keep covered while rolling the rotis so the dough does not dry out. Take one portion and roll into a smooth ball between your palms. Flatten the ball, turn over in the platter of atta and, using a rolling pin, roll out evenly to about 20cm (8in) in diameter.

Place a tava on medium heat and wait till it warms before transferring the rolled-out dough onto it. Turn over once or twice to roast evenly on both sides till light brown. Brush with ghee or butter. Repeat the process till all the rotis are ready. Serve hot.

Perfect when light brown and slightly crisp.

Palak ki roti

A very attractive, and delicious, green roti

Makes 6
Prep 1 hour
Cook 15–20 minutes

280g (9¾oz) spinach, finely chopped
70g (2¼oz) fresh coriander, minced
2–3 green chillies, minced
1 tsp ginger paste
1 tsp garlic paste
15g (½oz) coriander powder
1 tsp cumin seeds, roasted and ground
1 tsp salt
280g (9¾oz) atta (whole wheat flour)
15ml (½fl oz) ghee or 15g (½oz) butter, for brushing

PAIR IT WITH

KHATTA TAMATAR

Heat 10ml (¼fl oz) oil in a heavy-based pan and add 1 tsp cumin seeds. When they start to splutter, add ½ tsp asafoetida powder, 1 tsp fennel seeds, ¼ tsp turmeric powder, 30g (1oz) coriander powder, 245g (8½oz) tomatoes, cut into wedges, and 2 chopped green chillies (optional). Cover and cook on medium heat for 5 minutes. Add 140ml (4¾fl oz) water and cook for 10 minutes. Remove and sprinkle 30g (1oz) chopped fresh coriander. Serve hot.

Wash and drain the spinach well and place it in a heavy-based pan together with fresh coriander, green chillies, ginger paste, garlic paste, coriander powder, cumin seeds, and salt. Add about 70ml (2¼fl oz) of water and boil till the water dries out. Cool, then blend into a smooth paste.

Set aside 35g (1¼oz) of atta in a platter. Place the remaining atta in a deep bowl, add the spinach paste, and mix thoroughly. Slowly add about 35ml (1¼fl oz) of water while kneading the atta into a pliable dough that does not stick to your hand or the bowl. Cover with a thin muslin cloth and keep for 30 minutes.

Divide the dough into 6 equal portions and keep covered while rolling the rotis, so the dough does not dry out. Take one portion and roll into a smooth ball between your palms. Flatten the ball, turn over in the platter of atta, and, using a rolling pin, roll out evenly to about 20cm (8in) diameter.

Place a tava on medium heat and wait till it warms before transferring the rolled-out dough onto it. Turn over once or twice to roast both sides evenly. After both sides are roasted, turn the heat to low, wear an oven glove, and gently, but firmly, press the roti with your fingers while rotating it on the tava. This will puff up the roti to a certain extent. Brush with ghee or butter and serve hot.

Perfect when puffed up and has brown spots.

Methi roti

Flatbread made with slightly bitter fenugreek leaves is a popular favourite

Makes 6

Prep 1 hour

Cook 15–20 minutes

280g (9¾oz) atta (whole wheat flour)
70g (2¼oz) fenugreek leaves, minced
1 tsp cumin seeds, roasted and ground
2–3 green chillies, minced (optional)
30g (1oz) fresh coriander, minced
1 tsp salt
15ml (½fl oz) ghee or 15g (½oz) butter, for brushing

Set aside 35g (1¼oz) of atta in a platter. Place the remaining atta in a deep bowl, add the fenugreek leaves and all the other ingredients, including green chillies (if using), and mix well. Slowly add about 105ml (3½fl oz) of water while kneading the atta into a pliable dough that does not stick to your hand or the bowl. Cover with a thin muslin cloth and keep for 30 minutes.

Divide the dough into 6 equal portions. Remember to keep it covered while rolling the rotis so the dough does not dry out. Take one portion and roll into a smooth ball between your palms. Flatten the ball, turn over in the platter of atta and, using a rolling pin, roll out evenly to about 20cm (8in) in diameter.

Place a tava on medium heat and wait till warms before transferring the rolled-out dough onto it. Turn over once or twice to roast both sides evenly. After both sides are roasted, turn the heat to low, put on an oven glove, and firmly, but gently, press the roti with your fingers while rotating it on the tava. This will puff up the roti a little. Brush with ghee or butter and serve hot.

Perfect when covered with small, crispy, brown spots.

Thalipeeth

Spiced multigrain flatbread from Maharashtra

Makes 6
Prep 30 minutes
Cook 20–25 minutes

140g (5oz) atta (whole wheat flour)
70g (2¼oz) jowar atta (sorghum flour)
70g (2¼oz) besan (gram flour)
15g (½oz) bajra atta (pearl millet flour)
15g (½oz) urad chilka atta (black gram flour)
15g (½oz) thick flattened rice or poha
1½ tsp ginger paste
15g (½oz) coriander powder
10g (¼oz) cumin seeds, roasted and ground
10g (¼oz) red chilli powder
¼ tsp turmeric powder
2–3 green chillies, minced (optional)
70g (2¼oz) onion, minced
70g (2¼oz) fresh coriander, minced
1½ tsp salt
30ml (1fl oz) vegetable oil

Set aside 35g (1¼oz) of atta in a platter. Place the remaining atta and all the other flours in a deep bowl and mix well. Add the other ingredients, except the oil, and mix again. Slowly add about 140ml (4¾fl oz) of water while kneading the flour into a pliable dough that does not stick to your hand or the bowl. Cover with a thin muslin cloth and keep for 30 minutes.

Divide the dough into 6 equal portions and keep it covered while rolling the rotis so the dough does not dry out. Cover the rolling surface with aluminium foil and brush the foil with a little oil. Take one portion and roll into a smooth ball between your palms. Flatten the ball, turn over in the platter of atta, and place it on the foil. Roll out evenly with a rolling pin until about 20cm (8in) in diameter. Cut a small, approximately 2cm (½in), hole in the centre to prevent the thalipeeth from puffing up.

Place a tava on medium heat and wait till it warms, then pour ½ tsp of oil onto it. Gently lift the foil and turn over the thalipeeth onto the hot tava. Remove the foil. Roast evenly on both sides adding another ½ tsp of oil for 3–4 minutes until it develops golden-brown patches. Once the thalipeeth have been made, serve hot with pickle, raita *(see p20)*, or plain yoghurt.

Perfect when golden-brown with some darker, crispy patches.

Mung dal roti

The split green dal adds plant-based protein to this flatbread

Makes 6
Prep 40 minutes
Cook 20–25 minutes

280g (9¾oz) atta (whole wheat flour)
2 green chillies, minced (optional)
30g (1oz) fresh coriander, minced
1 tsp ginger paste
10g (¼oz) cumin seeds, roasted and ground
140g (5oz) split green gram, cooked
15ml (½fl oz) ghee or 15g (½oz) butter, for brushing

Set aside 35g (1¼oz) of atta in a platter. Place the remaining atta in a deep bowl. Add green chillies (if using), fresh coriander, ginger paste, and cumin seeds, and mix well. Since split green gram already has salt, there is no need to add more. Slowly add the split green gram while kneading the atta into a pliable dough that does not stick to your hand or the bowl. If required, add a little water. Cover with a thin muslin cloth and keep for 30 minutes.

Divide the dough into 6 equal portions. Make sure you keep it covered while rolling the rotis, so the dough does not dry out. Take one portion and roll into a smooth ball between your palms. Flatten the ball, turn over in the platter of atta and, using a rolling pin, roll out evenly to about 20cm (8in) in diameter.

Place a tava on medium heat and wait till it warms before transferring the rolled-out dough onto it. Turn over once or twice to roast both sides evenly till the roti turns golden-brown. Brush with ghee or butter and serve hot. Repeat the process till all the rotis are ready.

Perfect when a lovely golden-brown in colour.

PAIR IT WITH

DHANIYA-NARIYAL CHUTNEY

Grind 140g (5oz) fresh coriander, 70g (2¼oz) grated fresh coconut, 1-2 green chillies (optional), 1 tsp salt and 10g (¼oz) yoghurt to a fine paste in a mixer-grinder without adding any water at all. Do not use desiccated or green coconut. It is the flesh of the hard, brown, mature coconut that adds the flavour.

Lehsun ki roti

Spicy, with an extra aromatic edge of garlic

Makes 6
Prep 45 minutes
Cook 20–25 minutes

- 2 dry, whole red chillies (optional)
- 15g (½oz) garlic
- 1½ tsp salt
- 30g (1oz) yoghurt
- 280g (9¾oz) atta (whole wheat flour)
- 15ml (½fl oz) ghee or 15g (½oz) butter, for brushing

If using whole red chillies, soak them for 1 hour and drain well. Crush the garlic, red chillis, and salt together in a mortar and pestle, and then add the yoghurt to make a paste.

Set aside 35g (1¼oz) of atta in a platter. Place the remaining atta in a deep bowl and crumble in the garlic–chilli paste. Slowly add about 105ml (3½fl oz) of water while kneading the atta into a pliable dough, which does not stick to your hand or the bowl. If required, add a little water. Cover with a thin muslin cloth and keep for 30 minutes.

Divide the dough into 6 equal portions. Keep them covered while rolling the rotis so the dough does not dry out. Take one portion and roll into a smooth ball between your palms. Flatten the ball, turn over in the platter of atta, and, using a rolling pin, roll out evenly to about 20cm (8in) in diameter.

Place a tava on medium heat and wait till it warms before transferring the roti onto it. Turn over once or twice to roast both sides evenly. Brush with ghee or butter and serve hot.

Perfect when crisp and golden-brown.

Gur ki roti

The sweetness of melted jaggery and fragrant fennel make a perfect combination

Makes 6
Prep 15 minutes
Cook 20–25 minutes

140g (5oz) jaggery powder
280g (9¾oz) atta (whole wheat flour)
15g (½oz) fennel seeds, crushed
15ml (½fl oz) ghee
15g (½oz) butter or 15ml (½fl oz) ghee, for brushing

Dissolve the jaggery in 140ml (4½fl oz) of warm water and set aside to cool.

Set aside 35g (1¼oz) of atta in a platter. Place the remaining atta in a deep bowl, add the fennel seeds and crumble in the ghee. Slowly add the jaggery water while kneading the atta into a pliable dough that does not stick to your hand or the bowl. If required, add a little more water. Divide the dough into 6 equal portions. Remember to keep them covered with a thin muslin cloth while rolling the rotis, so the dough does not dry out.

Take one portion and roll into a smooth ball between your palms. Flatten the ball, turn over in the platter of atta and, using a rolling pin, roll out evenly to about 20cm (8in) in diameter. Place a tava on medium heat and wait till it warms before transferring the rolled-out dough onto it. Turn over once or twice to roast both sides evenly, making sure the roti does not stick to the tava. Brush with ghee or butter and serve hot. Repeat the process till all the rotis are ready.

Perfect when golden-brown and oozing jaggery.

Puran poli

A favoured offering to the gods during the festival season in Maharashtra

Makes 6
Prep 3 hours 30 minutes
Cook 15–20 minutes

280g (9¾oz) atta (whole wheat flour)
70g (2¼oz) maida (all-purpose flour)
30ml (1fl oz) ghee
½ tsp salt

For stuffing
140g (5oz) split chickpea lentils
10ml (¼fl oz) ghee
¼ tsp nutmeg powder
1 tsp green cardamom powder
1 tsp fennel powder
1 tsp ginger powder
105g (3½oz) jaggery

Soak the split chickpea lentils for 3 hours. Then wash and drain before placing in a pressure cooker with about 280ml (9½fl oz) of water. Close the lid and bring to full pressure on medium heat. Leave to cook for another 5 minutes before removing. Set aside to cool.

Heat 10ml (¼fl oz) of ghee in a pan on low heat and add the dry spices. Stir for a few seconds. Add the cooked lentils and jaggery powder and mix well – there should be very little water at this stage. Cook the mixture on low heat till it is absolutely dry. Set aside to cool.

Set aside 35g (1¼oz) of atta in a platter. Place the remaining flours in a deep bowl and crumble in 30ml (1fl oz) of ghee. Slowly add about 105ml (3½fl oz) of water while kneading the flours into a pliable dough, which does not stick to the hand or the bowl. Cover with a thin muslin cloth and keep for 30 minutes. When the mix has cooled, mash to a smooth consistency, divide into 6 equal portions, and set aside.

To make the poli, divide the dough into 6 equal portions. Cover these while rolling out the rotis so that the dough does not dry out. Take one portion and roll into a smooth ball between your palms. Flatten the ball, turn over in the platter of atta, and, with a rolling pin roll out evenly to about 10cm (4in) in diameter. Place one portion of the stuffing in the centre, lift the edges to make a pouch, enclose the mix, and close it. Flatten with the hand, then roll out, as thin as possible, turning on both sides using a little dry atta to cover any lentil mix if it is exposed.

Warm a tava and place the puran poli on it. Roast turning over once or twice while applying a little ghee, till it turns a golden-brown. Serve hot or at room temperature.

Perfect when thin, soft and flaky.

Koki

A delectable, sweeter version of the savoury flatbread from the Sindhi community

Makes 6
Prep 15 minutes
Cook 20–25 minutes

350g (12¼oz) atta (whole wheat flour)
105ml (3½fl oz) ghee
105g (3½oz) sugar

Reserve 35g (1¼oz) of atta in a platter and place the remaining atta in a deep bowl. Crumble 60ml (2fl oz) ghee and the sugar into the atta and knead it into a stiff dough, adding just enough water to bind it.

Divide the dough into 6 equal portions. Cover with a thin muslin cloth while rolling the kokis, so the dough does not dry out. Flatten the ball, turn over in the platter of atta and, using a rolling pin, roll out evenly to about 10cm (4in) in the diameter. Kokis are slightly thick. With a fork, lightly prick the surface of the koki in several places.

Place a tava on medium heat and wait till it warms before transferring the rolled-out dough onto it. Spread ¾ tsp ghee, turn over and spread another ¾ tsp of ghee. Roast both sides evenly, making sure the koki does not stick to the tava.

Repeat the process till all the kokis are ready. Serve hot, though they taste just as nice when they have cooled.

Perfect when crisp with a biscuit-like texture.

ROAST ON TAVA WITH GHEE

Introduction

The paratha is a variant of the traditional roti – the difference lies in the application of ghee or oil between layers while rolling and while cooking on the tava. The health-conscious may use virgin oils and refuse to be as generous in their use, but the paratha remains a firm favourite that just has to be indulged in. What's more, it seems that wherever you look, at every corner, be it a roadside vendor, dhaba on the highway, or restaurant, there is a paratha to tempt you. It is a great travel favourite – be it on the road, rail, or air, the paratha makes a regular appearance on the food tray. Today, the very popular kathi rolls (street-food wraps) are also often wrapped in thin parathas.

Unfortunately, in these health-conscious times, when "fat" has become a word synonymous with unhealthy, it has meant that parathas are looked upon by many as a harmful indulgence. This is a pity. Ultimately, the amount of fat used is in your hands. The recipes in this book give the optimum amount for a crisp paratha – it is a personal choice to use more or less. Some homes spread ghee between the layers and do away with it altogether while roasting on the tava – the result is a cross between a roti and a paratha, soft but not crisp. Others choose to use vegetable oils, olive oil, even margarine, instead of ghee. Whatever the method you chose, aficionados will tell you that unless cooked in ghee and served with a generous helping of butter, a paratha, stuffed, flavoured, or plain, is not a paratha at all.

It is amazing how, just like the roti, parathas vary from household to household, even though the basic ingredients, that is whole wheat flour, water, and ghee or oil, remain the same. The difference could be in the layering, or the shape – a square paratha with four layers, the triangular one with three – or perhaps, a pinch of salt added to the dough, or a little ghee to make the paratha even softer. This is just the plain paratha. When it comes to variations with more than just salt or ghee mixed in the dough, or stuffed parathas, there appears to be no end to inventiveness

When adding ingredients to the dough, the same rules apply for both rotis and parathas. The difference comes after the dough has been prepared, in the layering and cooking methods. For a really soft paratha, heat the tava on high initially and then reduce the temperature before placing the paratha on it. Roasting on medium heat yields the best results. If the heat is too high, the parathas will become tough and hard. If it is too low, they will be undercooked, chewy, and soft.

Roasting on the tava with ghee or oil slows down fermentation, which is why parathas last longer than rotis. Be sure to let them cool before storing them in a double-walled insulated container, otherwise the trapped heat can release moisture and make the parathas soggy. If you are refrigerating them, use foil or butter paper between each paratha to separate them, as the cooled-down ghee can cause them to stick to each other and make the layers flake off when one tries to separate them. Parathas can be reheated to original softness on the tava or in the microwave, much like rotis.

The stuffed paratha is an undisputed favourite for satisfying hunger and taste buds at any time of day. Paired with plain yoghurt, raita, or chutney, it becomes a complete, fulfilling meal. So, what should

Stuffed parathas are best eaten fresh. They do not store well and they cannot be reheated to their original crispness.

you keep in mind while making a stuffed paratha? One of the most important aspects is the water content of the stuffing. For example, raw tomatoes, which have high water content, cannot be added to a stuffing. Adding them can make the dough too sticky to handle, or cause the paratha to break or disintegrate while rolling as the tomatoes may release water.

Since cooked vegetables already contain salt, additional salt is generally unnecessary when using them as stuffing. If you prefer a saltier flavour, it is better to mix salt into the flour before kneading, rather than adding it directly to the stuffing. For uncooked vegetables such as cauliflower, it is best to mince them, sprinkle with a little salt, and let them sit for 10 minutes. The process will release excess water, which can then be squeezed out by gently pressing the cauliflower in a colander.

The second crucial aspect of making a stuffed paratha is achieving the right texture. A beginner attempting to use a stuffing mix that is not smooth may find it easier to follow a different method. Roll out two plain rotis, spread the stuffing on one, and cover it with the other roti. Press the edges together to seal them, then gently roll out the stuffed paratha, applying minimal pressure. This will help flatten and make it easier to roast.

Stuffed parathas are best eaten fresh. They do not store well, especially if stuffed with pre-cooked vegetables, and they cannot be reheated to their original crispness.

Flours of other grains and lentils can be used to make innovative parathas, whether mixed into the dough or used as stuffing. Such parathas are more commonly made in the eastern, western, and southern regions of the country where different types of flours are easily available.

In the state of Uttarakhand for example, the local legume gahat, or horse gram (*see p95*), which is very popular in the winter months, is also transformed into a stuffing for parathas. The sattu paratha (*see p98*), a well-known, popular breakfast food from eastern Uttar Pradesh and Bihar, traditionally used roasted flours of seven (*saat* hence sattu) grains and pulses in the mix for the stuffing. Today, what is generally available and sold as sattu is the more easily available roasted-chickpea flour. This only underlines the infallible versatility of the very popular "anytime" favourite – the paratha.

Plain paratha

A basic roasted flatbread, which can liven up even the simplest meal

Makes 6
Prep 40 minutes
Cook 25–30 minutes

280g (9¾oz) atta (whole wheat flour)
60ml (2fl oz) ghee

Having set aside 35g (1¼oz) of atta in a platter, place the remaining atta in a deep bowl. Slowly add about 105ml (3½fl oz) of water while kneading the atta into a pliable dough that does not stick to your hands or the bowl. Cover with a thin muslin cloth and keep for 30 minutes.

Divide the dough into 6 equal portions. Keep these covered with a thin muslin cloth while rolling the parathas so the dough does not dry out. Take 1 portion and roll it into a smooth ball between your palms. Flatten the ball under your fingers, turn it over in the platter of atta, and, using a rolling pin, roll out evenly to about 15–17cm (6–7in) in diameter. Apply 1 tsp of ghee on the whole surface. Fold in half, apply ½ tsp ghee, and fold again to make a triangle. This gives the paratha its characteristic layers. Turn over in the platter of atta and roll out once again to about 15–17cm (6–7in) equilaterally.

Place a tava on medium heat and wait till it warms before transferring the rolled-out paratha onto it. Roast till the paratha starts to blister, then turn over, and spread 1 tsp ghee on the surface. Turn over again and spread 1 tsp ghee on the other side. Flip again. Roast both sides evenly till golden-brown patches indicate that the paratha is crisp and well cooked. Take off the tava and serve hot.

Perfect when crispy and golden-brown.

PAIR IT WITH

GAJAR KA RAITA

Take 175g (6¼oz) of yoghurt. Whisk in 10g (¼oz) roasted and ground cumin seeds and 1 tsp salt. Add 105g (3½oz) grated carrots, 35g (1¼oz) minced spring onions, 35g (1¼oz) minced fresh coriander, 30g (1oz) roasted sesame seeds, and 2 minced green chillies (optional). Mix well and serve cold.

Lachha paratha

A layered paratha that just melts in the mouth

Makes 6
Prep 1 hour
Cook 25–30 minutes

280g (9¾oz) atta (whole wheat flour)
1 tsp salt
90ml (3fl oz) ghee

Reserve 35g (1¼oz) of atta in a platter and place the remaining atta and the salt in a deep bowl and mix. Add about 105ml (3½fl oz) of water while kneading the atta into a pliable dough that does not stick to your hands or the bowl. Cover with a thin muslin cloth and keep for 30 minutes.

Divide the dough into 6 equal portions. Keep the dough covered while rolling the parathas so that it does not dry out. Shape 1 portion to a smooth ball between your palms. Place it on the work surface and start rolling with your hands to form a long rope of about 2mm (0.08in) thickness. Spread 1 tsp ghee on the inner surface and wind the rope into a 5cm (2in) coil. Flatten the coil, turn over in the platter of atta, and roll out evenly to about 15–17cm (6–7in) in diameter.

Place a tava on medium heat and wait till it warms, then transfer the rolled-out paratha onto it. Roast till the paratha starts to blister, then turn over and spread 1 tsp ghee on the surface. Turn over and spread 1 tsp ghee to the other side. Roast both sides evenly till golden-brown patches indicate that the paratha is crisp and well cooked. Remove from the tava and serve hot.

Perfect when soft, flaky, and golden-brown.

Malabar parotta, with pakke aam ki curry

Buttery paratha and mango curry, a mouthwatering combination from the state of Kerala

Makes 6
Prep 1 hour
Cook 25–30 minutes

490g (17¼oz) maida (all-purpose flour)
1 tsp sugar
10g (¼oz) salt
175ml (6fl oz) milk
105ml (3½fl oz) vegetable oil

FOR PAKKE AAM KI CURRY
30ml (1fl oz) vegetable oil
1 tsp cumin seeds
2–3 whole red chillies
2–3 sprigs of curry leaves
420g (14¼oz) ripe mangoes, peeled and cut into 5-cm (2-in) pieces (seeds to be saved)
30g (1oz) sugar
105g (3½oz) coconut powder
1 tsp red chilli powder

Place the maida in a deep bowl and mix in the sugar and salt. Slowly add milk while kneading the maida into a pliable, non-sticky dough. Cover with a thin muslin cloth and keep for 15 minutes.

Knead the dough again for a couple of minutes, then divide it into 6 equal portions. Cover and rest the dough for another 10 minutes. Take 1 portion, leave the others covered so that they do not dry out, and shape into a smooth ball between your palms. Coat with 1 tsp oil, then flatten and roll out to about 20cm (8in) in diameter. Apply 1 tsp of oil and continue rolling out to as thin as possible. Try rolling evenly, but do not worry about any holes if they appear.

Place a tava to warm on medium heat. Gather the rolled-out dough in accordion folds to form one long strip. Wind the strip into a coil, press down to flatten it, apply ½ tsp oil, and roll out to about 15–17cm (6–7in) in diameter. Increase the heat and transfer the parotta onto the tava. Roast till the parotta starts to blister, then turn over, and spread ½ tsp oil on the surface. Turn over and apply ½ tsp oil to the other side. Roast both sides evenly till golden-brown patches indicate that the parotta is crisp and perfect. Remove from the tava. Malabar parotta is well done when it is flaky and golden-brown.

10g (¼oz) cumin seeds, roasted and ground
½ tsp turmeric powder
10g (¼oz) salt

To make the pakke aam ki curry, heat the oil in a heavy-based pan, and add the cumin seeds, whole red chillies, and curry leaves. When they start to splutter, add the mango pieces and the seeds, the remaining dry spices, and salt. Cook till the mangoes are really soft, almost mushy, then add the sugar. As mangoes vary in sweetness, the key is to get the perfect balance of the salt, sugar, and chilli. Keep stirring till the sugar dissolves, then add the coconut powder, and leave to simmer for 2 minutes. Serve hot with Malabar parotta.

Mooli paratha

A spiced paratha stuffed with grated white radish for irresistible tangy spiciness

Makes 6
Prep 40 minutes
Cook 25–30 minutes

350g (12¼oz) atta (whole wheat flour)
60ml (2fl oz) ghee
1 tsp salt

For stuffing
300g (10oz) white radish
1 tsp salt
30g (1oz) fresh coriander, minced
10g (¼oz) red chilli powder
10g (¼oz) cumin seeds, roasted and ground
10g (¼oz) raw mango powder

Peel the white radish and cut off the stem and tip. Wash and grate with a fine grater. Place the grated radish in a bowl, add 1 tsp of salt, and set aside for 10 minutes.

Set aside 35g (1¼oz) of atta in a platter. Place the remaining atta in a deep bowl, add 1 tsp of salt, and mix well. Slowly add about 140ml (4¾fl oz) water while kneading the atta into a pliable dough that does not stick to your hands or the bowl. Cover with a thin muslin cloth and keep for 30 minutes.

Squeeze the radish to drain the excess water. Add the other ingredients for the stuffing, mix thoroughly, divide into 6 equal portions, and set aside.

To make the parathas, divide the dough into 6 equal portions. Remember to keep these covered while rolling the parathas so the dough does not dry out. Take 1 portion and roll into a smooth ball between your palms. Flatten the ball under your fingers, turn over in the platter of atta, and, using a rolling pin, roll out evenly to about 13cm (5in) in diameter. Apply 1 tsp of ghee on the surface. Place one portion of the stuffing in the centre of the rolled-out dough, lift the edges to make a pouch, enclose the mix, and seal the pouch. Gently flatten the pouch, turn over in the platter of atta, and roll out to about 17cm (7in) in diameter, making sure to flip and roll on both sides. Use a little dry atta to cover any radish mix, if exposed.

Place a tava on medium heat and wait till it warms before transferring the rolled-out paratha onto it. Roast till the paratha starts to blister, then turn over, and spread 1 tsp ghee on the surface. Turn over and spread 1 tsp ghee on the other side. Flip again. Roast both sides evenly till golden-brown patches indicate that the paratha is crisp and well cooked. Remove from the tava and serve hot.

Perfect when a crisp casing reveals a soft and moist filling.

Aloo paratha

May be called the classic stuffed paratha, which has a spiced potato filling

Makes 6
Prep 45 minutes
Cook 25–30 minutes

350g (12¼oz) atta (whole wheat flour)
60ml (2fl oz) ghee

For stuffing
250g (8¾oz) potatoes, boiled
1½ tsp red chilli powder
10g (¼oz) cumin seeds, roasted and ground
10g (¼oz) raw mango powder
1½ tsp salt
30g (1oz) fresh coriander, minced
10g (¼oz) fresh mint, minced

Peel and crumble the potatoes, add the dry spices, fresh coriander, fresh mint, and salt, and mash to a smooth consistency. Divide the mix into 6 equal portions and set aside.

Set aside 35g (1¼oz) of atta in a platter. Place the remaining atta in a deep bowl, slowly add about 140ml (4¾fl oz) water while kneading the atta into a pliable dough that does not stick to your hands or the bowl. Cover with a thin muslin and keep for 30 minutes.

Divide the dough into 6 equal portions. Keep these covered while rolling the parathas so the dough does not dry out. Take 1 portion and roll into a smooth ball between your palms. Flatten the ball under your fingers, turn over in the platter of atta, and, using a rolling pin, roll out evenly to about 10cm (4in) in diameter. Place 1 portion of the stuffing in the centre of the rolled-out dough, lift the edges to make a pouch, enclose the mix, and seal the pouch. Gently flatten the pouch, turn over in the platter of atta, and roll out to about 17cm (7in) in diameter, making sure to turn and roll on both sides. Use a little dry atta to cover any mix if exposed.

Place a tava on medium heat and wait till it warms before transferring the rolled-out paratha onto it. Roast till the paratha starts to blister, then turn over and spread 1 tsp ghee on the surface. Turn over and apply 1 tsp ghee to the other side. Flip again. Roast both sides evenly till golden-brown patches indicate that the paratha is crisp and well cooked. Remove from the tava and serve hot.

Perfect when crispy outside with creamy, spicy aloo inside.

Gahat ki dal ka paratha

A local stuffed paratha from Uttarakhand with horse gram filling

Makes 6
Prep 1 hour
Cook 25–30 minutes

350g (12¼oz) atta (whole wheat flour)
1 tsp salt
60ml (2fl oz) ghee

For stuffing

210g (7½oz) horse gram, washed and soaked overnight
100g (3½oz) onions, minced
3–4 garlic cloves
10g (¼oz) ginger paste
¼ tsp turmeric powder
10g (¼oz) red chilli powder
30g (1oz) coriander powder
1 tsp asafoetida powder
1 tsp raw mango powder
1½ tsp salt
30g (1oz) fresh coriander, minced

Drain the horse gram and place in a pressure cooker with all the stuffing ingredients. Add about 210ml (7½fl oz) water, bring to full pressure on medium heat, and cook for 15 more minutes. When cooled, drain excess water and mash well until smooth. Divide into 6 equal portions and set aside.

Reserve 35g (1¼oz) of atta in a platter and place the remaining atta in a deep bowl and mix well. Slowly add about 140ml (4¾fl oz) water, while kneading the atta into a pliable dough that does not stick to your hands or the bowl. Divide the dough into 6 equal portions. Cover with a thin muslin cloth while rolling the parathas.

Take 1 portion and roll into a smooth ball between your palms. Flatten the ball under your fingers, turn over in the platter of atta, and, using a rolling pin, roll out to about 10cm (4in) in diameter. Place a portion of the horse gram mix in the centre of the rolled-out dough, lift the edges to make a pouch, enclose the mix, and seal the pouch. Gently flatten, turn over in the platter of atta, and roll out to about 17cm (7in) in diameter, making sure to turn and roll on both sides. Use a little dry atta to cover any mix if exposed.

Place a tava on medium heat and once warm, transfer the rolled-out paratha onto it. Roast till the paratha starts to blister, then turn over, and spread 1 tsp ghee on the surface. Turn over and spread 1 tsp ghee on the other side. Flip again. Roast both sides evenly till golden-brown patches appear. Remove from the tava and serve hot.

Perfect when dry and flaky inside.

Gobi paratha

A winter favourite, with a hearty filling of fresh, spiced cauliflower

Makes 6
Prep 40 minutes
Cook 25–30 minutes

350g (12¼oz) atta (whole wheat flour)
60ml (2fl oz) ghee

For stuffing

210g (7½oz) large cauliflower florets
1½ tsp salt
30g (1oz), fresh coriander, minced
15g (½oz) fresh mint, minced
2–3 green chillies, minced (optional)
1 tsp cumin, roasted and ground
1 tsp ginger paste

Set aside 35g (1¼oz) of atta in a platter and place the remaining atta in a deep bowl. Slowly add about 140ml (4¾fl oz) water while kneading the atta into a pliable dough that does not stick to your hands or the bowl. Cover with a thin muslin cloth and keep for 30 minutes.

Wash and drain the cauliflower. Finely grate the florets. Add 1 tsp of salt and set aside for 15 minutes. Drain the grated cauliflower and mix the remaining ingredients and the salt into it. Rub in well to enhance the flavours. Then divide into 6 equal portions

To make the parathas, divide the dough into 12 equal portions. Cover these while rolling the parathas so the dough does not dry out. Take 1 portion and roll into a smooth ball between your palms. Flatten the ball under your fingers, turn over in the platter of atta, and, using a rolling pin, roll out evenly to about 13cm (5in) in diameter. Repeat with another portion of the dough. Spread 1 portion of the cauliflower on one, and carefully cover it with the other rolled-out paratha. Press down on the edges to seal them. Gently roll out to about 15–17cm (6–7in) in diameter, taking care not to break the dough.

Place a tava on medium heat and wait till it warms before transferring the rolled-out paratha onto it. Roast till the paratha starts to blister, then turn over, and spread 1 tsp ghee on the surface. Turn over and spread 1 tsp ghee on the other side. Flip again. Roast both sides evenly till golden-brown patches indicate that the paratha is crisp and well cooked. Remove from the tava and serve hot.

Perfect when the cauliflower stuffing is soft and juicy.

Paneer paratha

Spicy and flavourful breakfast favourite

Makes 6
Prep 45 minutes
Cook 20–25 minutes

350g (12¼oz) atta (whole wheat flour)
60ml (2fl oz) ghee

For stuffing
210g (7½oz) paneer
30g (1oz) fresh coriander, minced
2–3 green chillies, minced (optional)
10g (¼oz) cumin seeds, roasted and ground
1 tsp garam masala
1½ tsp salt

Set aside 35g (1¼oz) of atta in a platter and place the remaining atta in a deep bowl. Slowly add about 140ml (4¾fl oz) water while kneading the atta into a pliable dough that does not stick to your hands or the bowl. Cover with a thin muslin cloth and keep for 30 minutes.

Place the paneer in a bowl, add all the ingredients for the stuffing, and mix to a smooth consistency. Divide the mix into 6 equal portions and set aside.

To make the parathas, divide the dough into 6 equal portions. Remember to cover them while rolling the parathas so the dough does not dry out. Take 1 portion and roll into a smooth ball between your palms. Flatten the ball under your fingers, turn over in the platter of atta, and, using a rolling pin, roll out evenly to about 10cm (4in) in diameter. Place one portion of the paneer mix in the centre of the rolled-out dough, lift the edges to make a pouch, enclose the mix, and seal the dough pouch. Gently flatten the pouch, turn over in the platter of atta, and roll out to about 17cm (7in) in diameter, making sure to turn on both sides. Use a little dry atta to cover any paneer mix if exposed.

Place a tava on medium heat and after it warms, transfer the rolled-out paratha onto it. Roast till the paratha starts to blister, then turn over, and spread 1 tsp ghee on the surface. Turn over and spread 1 tsp ghee to the other side. Flip again. Roast both sides evenly till golden-brown patches appear. Take off the tava and serve hot.

Perfect when the moist filling perfectly complements the crisp casing.

Sattu paratha

The traditional breakfast speciality from the states of Bihar and Uttar Pradesh

Makes 6
Prep 45 minutes
Cook 25–30 minutes

350g (12¼oz) atta (whole wheat flour)
60ml (2fl oz) ghee
1 tsp salt

For stuffing
1½ tsp salt
210g (7½oz) onions, minced
210g (7½oz) sattu (roasted chickpea flour)
45g (1½oz) fresh coriander, minced
1½ tsp ginger paste
10g (¼oz) red chilli powder
10g (¼oz) cumin powder
1 tsp raw mango powder

PAIR IT WITH

NIMBU–ADRAK ACHAR

Place 140g (5oz) ginger either julienned or grated coarsely, 2 green chillies slit lengthwise, and 15g (½oz) of salt in a clean and dry airtight bottle. Add the juice of 6-8 lemons, making sure the ginger is well covered. Close the bottle, shake to mix well, and keep aside. In hot weather, the pickle requires only a day to be ready to eat, but when it is cold it may take up to 3 days.

Rub a little salt into the onions to remove excess water and set aside for 10 minutes.

Set aside 35g (1¼oz) of atta in a platter and place the remaining atta and salt in a deep bowl. Slowly add about 140ml (4¾fl oz) water while kneading the atta into a pliable dough, which does not stick to your hands or the bowl. Cover with a thin muslin cloth and keep for 30 minutes.

Drain and lightly squeeze the onions, add the stuffing ingredients and remaining salt, and mix well. The stuffing should be a little sticky. Divide into 6 equal portions, cover, and set aside.

To make the parathas, divide the dough into 6 equal portions. Cover while rolling the parathas. Take 1 portion and roll into a smooth ball between your palms. Flatten the ball with your fingers, turn over in the platter of atta, and roll out evenly to about 13cm (5in) in diameter with a rolling pin. Brush the surface with 1 tsp ghee. Place 1 portion of the sattu mix in the centre, lift the edges to make a pouch, enclose it, and seal. Gently flatten the pouch, turn over in the platter of sattu atta, and roll out to about 17cm (7in) in diameter, turning on both sides. Use a little dry atta to cover any sattu mix if exposed.

Place a tava on medium heat and wait till it warms before transferring the rolled-out paratha onto it. Roast till the paratha starts to blister, then turn over, and spread 1 tsp ghee on the surface. Turn over and spread 1 tsp ghee to the other side. Flip again. Roast both sides evenly till golden-brown patches appear. Remove from the tava and serve hot.

Perfect when the ghee is fully absorbed resulting in a soft and moist paratha.

Sidu

A stuffed, leavened bread from the state of Himachal Pradesh

Makes 6
Prep 1 hour
Rest 2–3 hours
Cook 1 hour 30 minutes

280g (9¾oz) atta (whole wheat flour)
10g (¼oz) dry yeast
1 tsp salt
1 tsp sugar
15ml (½fl oz) ghee

For stuffing
140g (5oz) walnuts, shelled
1 tsp ginger paste
1 tsp garlic paste
100g (3½oz) onions, chopped
2–3 green chillies, chopped (optional)

Add yeast and sugar in 70ml (2¼fl oz) of warm water, mix, and rest for 15 minutes.

Set aside 35g (1¼oz) atta in a platter. In a deep bowl, mix salt with the remaining atta, add the yeast mix, and slowly knead the atta into a pliable dough that does not stick to your hands or the bowl. Cover and keep till it doubles in size.

Grind the walnuts, ginger, garlic, onions, and green chillies (if using), without using water, and set aside.

Divide the dough into 6 equal portions. Cover with a thin muslin cloth so that it does not dry out while you are rolling the sidu. Take 1 portion and shape it into a smooth ball between your palms. Flatten and roll out evenly to about 23cm (9in) in diameter. Spread 45g (1½oz) of the walnut mix on one side of the rolled-out dough. Fold the other side to cover the stuffing and press the edges to seal well. Make all 6 sidu.

Steam for about 15–20 minutes or till a knife comes out clear after inserting it into the side. Warm a tava on medium heat, spread ½ tsp of ghee on each side and roast the steamed sidu for about 5–7 minutes, turning over once so that both sides turn a nice golden-brown. Serve hot.

Perfect when a knife inserted comes out clean.

Anda paratha

A popular street food in northern India, featuring a savoury egg filling

Makes 6
Prep 45 minutes
Cook 25–30 minutes

350g (12¼oz) atta (whole wheat flour)
60ml (2fl oz) ghee

For stuffing

3 eggs
100g (3½oz) onions, minced
2–3 green chillies (optional)
30g (1oz) fresh coriander, minced
15g (½oz) coriander powder
10g (¼oz) garam masala
1 tsp black pepper powder
1½ tsp salt

Set aside the usual 35g (1¼oz) of atta in a platter. Place the remaining atta in a deep bowl and slowly add about 140ml (4¾fl oz) of water, while kneading the atta into a pliable, non-sticky dough. Cover and keep for 30 minutes.

Crack the eggs into a bowl, beat well, mix in all the other stuffing ingredients, and set aside.

To make the parathas, divide the dough into 12 equal portions. Cover with a thin muslin cloth while rolling the parathas so the dough does not dry out. Take 1 portion and shape it to a smooth ball between your palms. Flatten, turn over in the platter of atta, and roll out evenly to about 15–17cm (6–7in) in diameter. Repeat with another portion of the dough.

Place a tava on medium heat and wait till it warms before placing one rolled-out paratha on it. Wait till the paratha warms a little, then spread 2–3 tbsp of the egg mix evenly over the surface. Reduce the heat and cover with a lid for 30 seconds. Remove the lid and carefully place the second paratha on top of the first, pressing down on the edges to seal them. Spread 1 tsp ghee on the surface and cover again for a minute. Remove the lid, turn over gently, and spread 1 tsp ghee on the other side, and turn over again. Roast both sides evenly till golden-brown patches indicate that the paratha is crisp and well cooked. Remove from the tava and serve hot.

Perfect when the egg filling is light, fluffy, and fully set.

Keema paratha

A meat version starring minced chicken as the key ingredient

Makes 6
Prep: 1 hour
Cook: 25–30 minutes

350g (12¼oz) atta (whole wheat flour)
60ml (2fl oz) ghee

For stuffing
280g (9¾oz) chicken, minced
100g (3½oz) onion, minced
30g (1oz) ginger-garlic paste
¼ tsp turmeric powder
10g (¼oz) cumin seeds, roasted and ground
10g (¼oz) garam masala
15g (½oz) coriander powder
10g (¼oz) red chilli powder
1½ tsp salt
30g (1oz) fresh coriander, minced

PAIR IT WITH

PYAAZ–TAMATAR RAITA

Take 140g (5oz) yoghurt. Whisk in 1 tsp each of red chilli powder, roasted and ground cumin seeds, and salt, along with ¼ tsp of asafoetida powder (optional). Add 70g (2¼oz) each of minced tomatoes and onions, 30g (1oz) minced fresh coriander, and 2 minced green chillies (optional). Mix well and serve cold.

Place all the ingredients for the stuffing, except the fresh coriander, into a pressure cooker and mix well. Add 140ml (4¾fl oz) water, close the lid, bring to full pressure on medium heat, and leave to cook for another 15 minutes. Set aside to cool.

Reserve 35g (1¼oz) of atta in a platter and place the rest in a deep bowl. Slowly add about 140ml (4¾fl oz) water while kneading the atta into a pliable dough, which does not stick to your hand or the bowl. Cover and keep for 30 minutes.

Open the pressure cooker and on low heat, dry out the minced chicken, almost to the point where it begins to stick to the bottom. Transfer to a bowl, add the fresh coriander, and mix well. When cooled, divide into 6 equal portions and set aside.

To make the paratha, divide the dough into 6 equal portions. Cover with a thin muslin cloth so the dough does not dry out. Take one portion and shape into a smooth ball between your palms. Flatten, turn over in the platter of atta, and roll out evenly to about 10cm (4in) in diameter. Place 1 portion of the minced mix in the centre of the rolled-out dough, lift the edges to make a pouch, enclose the mix, and seal. Gently flatten the pouch, turn over in the platter of atta, and roll out to about 17cm (7in) in diameter, making sure to turn on both sides. Dust any exposed mix with dry atta.

Place a tava on medium heat and wait till it warms before transferring the rolled-out paratha on it. Roast till the paratha starts to blister, then turn over, and spread 1 tsp ghee on the surface. Turn over and spread 1 tsp ghee on the other side. Flip again. Roast both sides evenly till golden-brown patches indicate that the paratha is crisp and well cooked. Remove from the tava and serve hot.

Perfect when the keema filling is soft inside a crisp paratha.

Virudhunagar parotta

A roasted and shallow-fried speciality from the city of Virudhunagar in Tamil Nadu

Makes 6
Prep 40 minutes
Cook 1 hour

280g (9¾oz) maida (all-purpose flour)
105ml (3½fl oz) vegetable oil
1 tsp salt

Set aside 35g (1¼oz) maida in a platter and place the remaining maida in a deep bowl. Add 15ml (½fl oz) vegetable oil and the salt and mix well. Then slowly pour in about 105ml (3½fl oz) of water while kneading the maida into a pliable dough that does not stick to your hands or the bowl. Cover with a thin muslin cloth and keep for 30 minutes. Knead again and keep for another 5 minutes. Divide the dough into 6 equal portions. Cover these while rolling the parathas so the dough does not dry out.

Take 1 portion and roll into a smooth ball between your palms. Flatten the ball under your fingers, turn over in the platter of maida, and, using a rolling pin, roll out evenly as thin as possible. With your hands, roll the flat roti to form a long rope of about 2mm (⅛in) thickness. Coil this rope to make a spiral. Flatten the coil under your fingers, turn over in the platter of maida, and using a rolling pin, roll out to about 13cm (5in) in diameter.

Place a tava on medium heat and wait until it warms before transferring the rolled-out paratha onto it. Half roast, turning over once or twice. Remove from the tava and set aside. Repeat with the remaining portions until all the parathas are half-cooked. Heat the remaining oil on medium heat in a flat, heavy-based pan, taking care that it does not become smoking hot. Shallow fry each parotta until crisp and serve hot.

Perfect when lovely deep golden-brown and crisp.

Meetha paratha

A sweet paratha that is a comforting favourite and a nostalgic childhood treat

Makes 6
Prep 40 minutes
Cook 40 minutes

280g (9¾oz) atta (whole wheat flour)
60ml (2fl oz) ghee
90g (3oz) sugar

Set aside 35g (1¼oz) atta in a platter, and in a deep bowl, knead the remaining atta into a pliable, non-sticky dough by slowly adding about 105ml (3½fl oz) of water in stages. Cover and keep for 30 minutes.

Divide the dough into 6 equal portions. Cover with a thin muslin cloth while rolling the parathas so the dough does not dry out. Shape 1 portion of the dough into a smooth ball between your palms. Flatten, turn over in the platter of atta, and roll out evenly to about 15–17cm (6–7in) in diameter. Apply 1 tsp ghee on the whole surface. Sprinkle 15g (½oz) sugar uniformly over the paratha, pressing it in lightly with the rolling pin. Fold in half, apply ½ tsp ghee, and fold again to make a triangle. This will create a layered effect. Turn over in the platter of atta and roll out once again to about 15–17cm (6–7in) equilaterally.

Place a tava on medium heat and wait till it warms before placing the rolled-out paratha onto it. Roast till the paratha starts to blister, then turn over, and spread 1 tsp ghee on the surface. Turn over and spread 1 tsp ghee on the other side. Flip again. Roast both sides evenly, taking care not to burn the sugar, till golden-brown patches indicate that the paratha is crisp and well cooked. Remove from the tava and serve hot.

Perfect when crispy golden-brown outside with melted sugar inside.

BAKE IN THE OVEN

Introduction

The most popular Indian fermented breads are kulchas and naans. Unlike rotis and parathas, which are primarily made from whole wheat flour, these are made from refined (all-purpose) flour. Moreover, these fermented breads were traditionally baked in the tandoor.

There was a time when the tandoor had a place in many kitchens of northern India – the urban metropolis of Delhi was no exception. Those residential areas that did not have a tandoor could still get freshly baked tandoori breads. For a small fee, a lady would come around every day and take the required dough from each household. She would then bake the specified breads in her tandoor and deliver them.

Not only does the modern kitchen rarely have place for a coal-fired tandoor, today access to a tandoor has also become a thing of the past. Fortunately, it is possible to bake these breads at home in the oven. The basic method remains the same, the only significant loss being the smoky flavour imparted by an open fire. The kulcha can also be made on the tava, as detailed in this section.

Since refined flour is being used, the dough has to be kneaded well, until it no longer sticks to the hand. After kneading the dough, it must be set aside to ferment – the duration depends on the ambient temperature, but indicative times are mentioned in the recipes. In cooler conditions, covering the dough with a warm cloth will help in fermentation.

The inclusion of oil or butter in the dough should prevent it from sticking while rolling. If it does stick, the work surface can be lightly dusted with dry flour. After rolling out the dough, the process of baking in the oven is similar to that of baking in a tandoor. The side of the bread that will come in contact with the baking tray of the oven must be moistened before being put in. Except for some of the thicker, special breads, turning over to ensure even cooking is not needed as both sides cook simultaneously. The ideal oven temperatures are mentioned in each

At home, and without a tandoor, it is possible to bake these breads in the oven, with the only significant loss being the smoky flavour imparted by an open fire.

recipe. It is important to know that the microwave is not suitable for this type of cooking.

Fermented breads can also be made with ingredients in the dough, or stuffed, in much the same way as rotis and parathas. However, other than the plain kulcha, these breads cannot be reheated. Whether on the tava or in the oven, reheating destroys their flavour and texture, making them almost too tough to chew.

Of all Indian breads, it is perhaps the kulcha that is the least known outside the subcontinent. Usually eaten with chana (*see pp176–177*) or matra (*see pp120–121*), it is very popular in North India and, as with other breads, its popularity has led to many innovations. Until recently, the kulcha was a flat and light bread, neither very thick nor fluffy. While street food stalls still serve the traditional flat kulcha, fluffy kulchas with a whole range of toppings can now be seen in many bakeries, competing with the variety of breads available. Stuffed kulchas are also a recent addition, with potato and split chickpea lentil fillings being the favourites.

Plain kulchas can be stored the same way as you would store parathas. They can be kept in the fridge for up to two days. The best way to reheat them is in the microwave. Place a paper napkin in a microwave dish. Take a couple of kulchas – do not heat too many at one time – sprinkle a few drops of water between each, place another paper napkin on top, then cover with a microwave suitable lid, and heat for one minute. Let them rest for a minute or so before serving. Stuffed kulchas do not store well.

The naan, which has quietly held its own for at least 600 years if not more, is perhaps the most widely known and popular tandoori bread. This is not to say it has not undergone changes and modifications. Though the tandoor may have lost its place in the larger domestic framework, there are many chefs who continue to study its concepts and master the technique of cooking in it, producing an unlimited variety of the most innovative and soul-satisfying breads. In addition, the thrill of watching an expert tandoori cook in action has secured the tandoor's place in today's "open-kitchen" restaurants.

While the classic naan, with its traditional pairing of vegetarian and meat curries, still stands firm in its position as leading favourite, a variety of stuffed naans have become mainstream and are in great demand. As with rotis and parathas, any cooked vegetable or a mince of chicken or mutton can be used as stuffing for naans. Sprinkling chopped fresh mint, sesame seeds, nigella seeds, melon seeds, fresh coriander, ginger slivers, and green chillies on top just before baking greatly enhances the flavours. Once again, you need to keep in mind that using tomato or any watery vegetable as stuffing is an absolute no.

In addition to these better-known breads, different parts of the country bake their own unique breads. For example, of the many breads baked in the northern region of Kashmir, the lavasa (*see pp124–125*), an everyday fermented flatbread, slightly resembles the kulcha. The tsot, a small biscuit-like bread, about 10–12cm (4–5in) in diameter is a breakfast favourite (*see pp136–137*). Both of these can be baked in the oven.

The Rajasthani baati (*see p132*) and the litti (*see p138*) from Bihar, were not traditionally cooked in a tandoor but within a cow-dung cake fire. The method given in this book, details how to bake them in the oven at home.

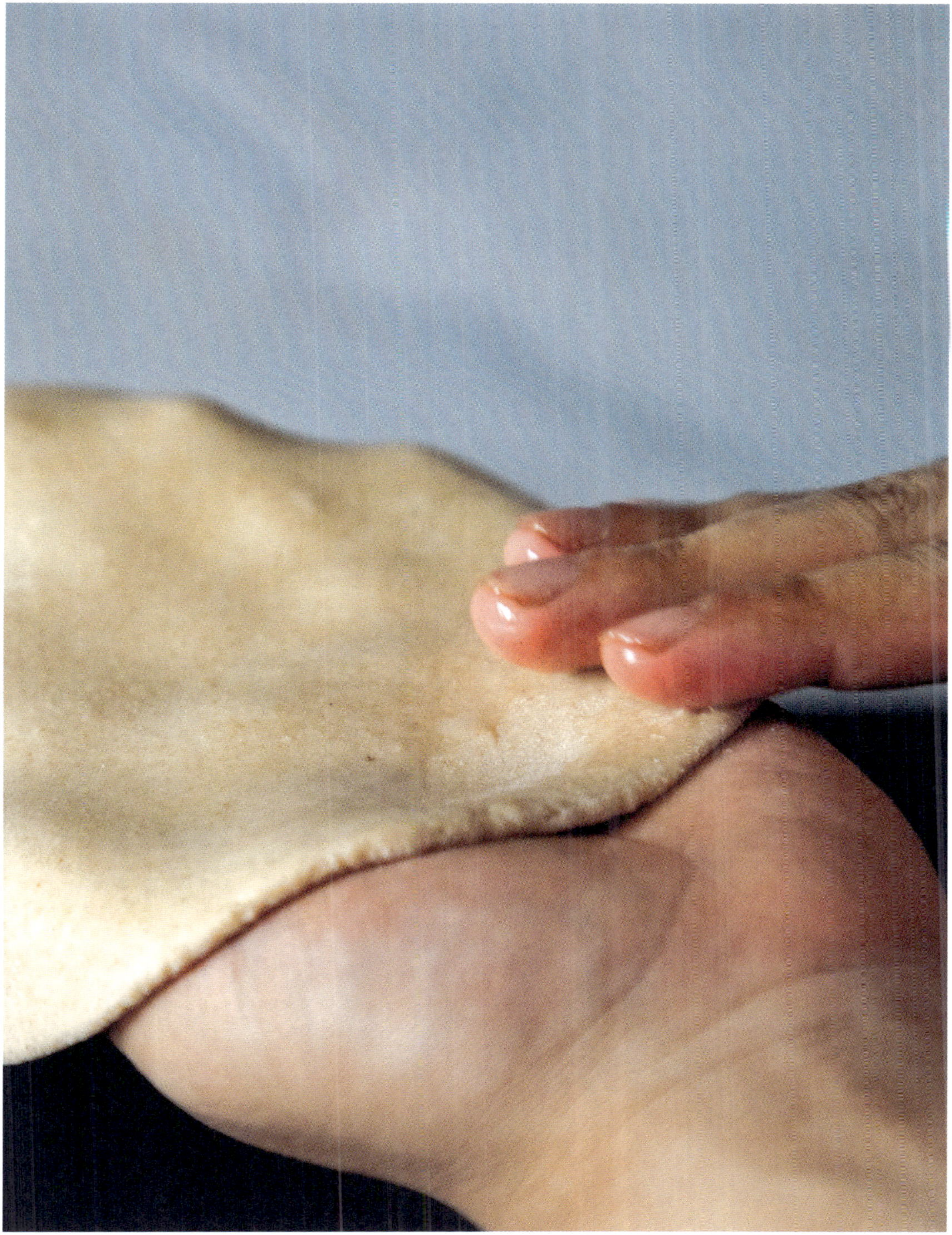

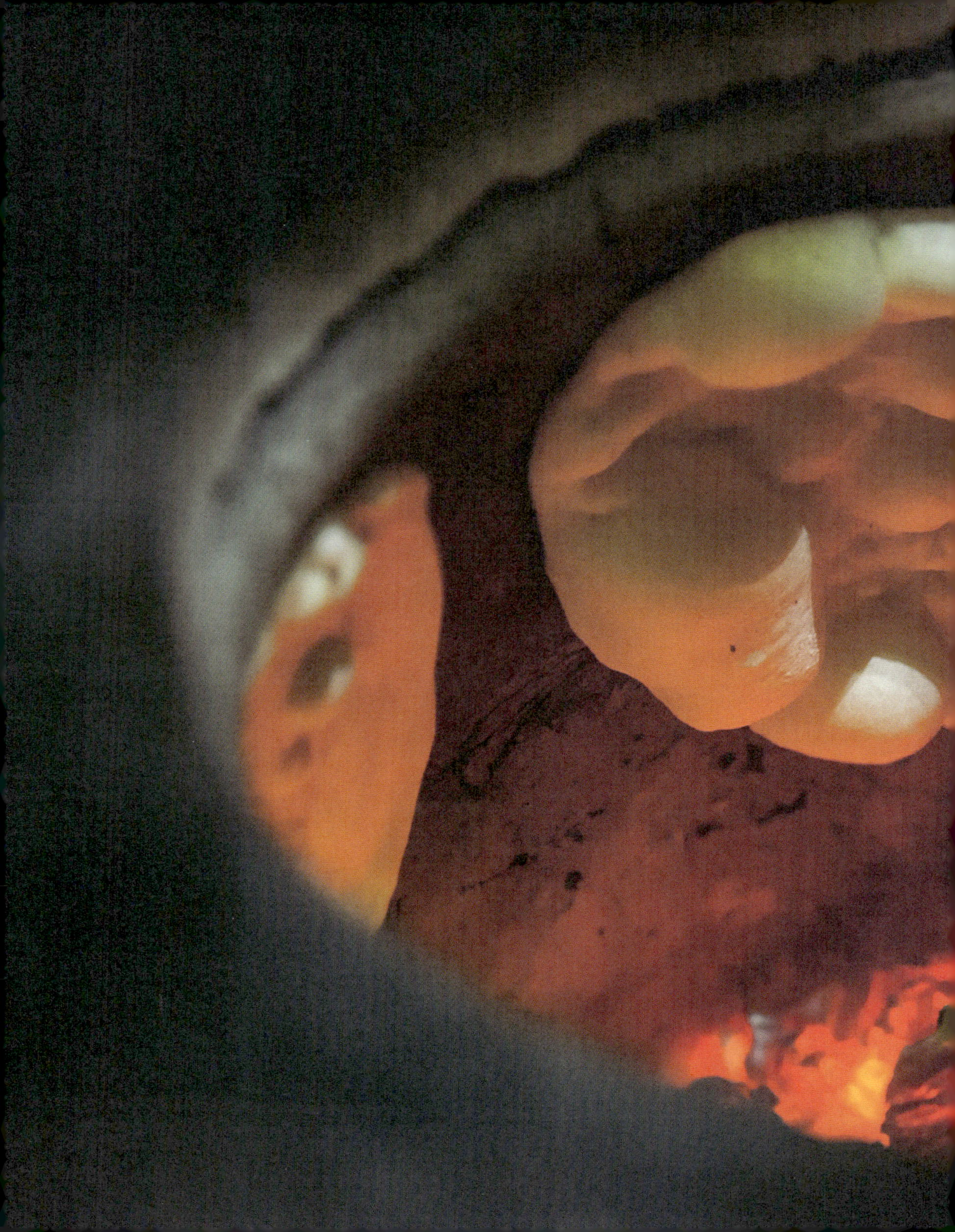

Tandoori roti

The difference in the taste and texture of a baked roti is quite surprising

Makes 6
Prep 45 minutes
Cook 15–20 minutes

280g (9¾oz) atta (whole wheat flour)
1 tsp salt
10ml (¼fl oz) vegetable oil

Set aside 35g (1¼oz) atta in a platter and place the remaining atta, salt, and oil in a deep bowl. Slowly add about 105ml (3½fl oz) of water while kneading a pliable dough that does not stick to your hands or the bowl. Cover and keep for 30 minutes.

Preheat the oven, then divide the dough into 6 equal portions, and cover again so that the dough does not dry out while you are rolling the roti. Take 1 portion and shape it into a smooth ball between your palms. Flatten it under your fingers, turn over in the platter of atta, and roll out to about 15cm (6in) in diameter.

Brush off all the dry atta, wet your palms with water, and moisten both sides of the roti. Place the roti on the baking tray and bake for 5–6 minutes at 180°C (350°F) till brown spots appear on one side. Remove and serve hot.

If your oven is big enough, roll 3–4, moisten lightly, and place them on the tray in one go.

Perfect when crisp outside and chewy inside.

Kulcha, with matra

A popular street food featuring leavened flatbread and tangy, white peas

Makes 6
Prep 15 minutes
Rest 4 hours
Cook 15–20 minutes

280g (9¾oz) maida (all-purpose flour)
1 tsp salt
1 tsp baking powder
30ml (1fl oz) melted butter
30g (1oz) yoghurt
15ml (½fl oz) ghee or 15g (½oz) butter to serve

For garnish
60g (2oz) fresh coriander, minced
45g (1½oz) ginger, slivered
10g (¼oz) cumin seeds, roasted and ground
10g (¼oz) raw mango powder
1 tsp salt

Having set aside 35g (1¼oz) maida in a platter, place the remaining maida in a deep bowl. Mix in salt and baking powder, then crumble in the melted butter. Add the yoghurt and, while slowly adding 105ml (3½fl oz) water, knead until the dough is smooth and somewhat spongy. Cover with a thin damp muslin cloth and set aside for 4 hours.

Knead the risen dough again for a few minutes, then divide into 6 equal portions. Keep the dough covered with a thin muslin cloth while rolling the kulchas so that it does not dry out.

Mix all the ingredients for the garnish and set aside. Place a tava to warm on medium heat. Take 1 portion of dough and shape it into a smooth ball between your palms. Flatten it, turn over in the platter of maida, and roll out evenly to about 15cm (6in) in diameter. Sprinkle a little garnish on top of the kulcha and press it lightly into the dough with the rolling pin. Brush the other side of the kulcha with a little water and place it, moist side down, on the warm tava. Cover and cook on low heat for a couple of minutes. Sprinkle with a little water and turn over. The kulchas are perfect when light and fluffy.

Brush the kulchas with ½ tsp ghee or butter for added flavour.

FOR MATRA

105g (3½oz) matra (dried white peas), soaked overnight
1 tsp salt
¼ tsp turmeric powder
15ml (½fl oz) vegetable oil
1–2 bay leaves
15g (½oz) ginger-garlic paste
100g (3½oz) onions, sliced
1 tsp garam masala
1 tsp cumin seeds, roasted and ground
1 tsp raw mango powder
15g (½oz) coriander powder

For garnish

50g (1¾oz) tomatoes, finely chopped
30g (1oz) fresh coriander, chopped
2 green chillies, slit lengthwise (optional)
15g (½oz) ginger, julienned
30ml (1fl oz) lemon juice

Drain the matra and place in a pressure cooker with salt, a pinch of turmeric powder, and 280ml (9½fl oz) of water. Close the lid and bring to full pressure on medium heat, then allow to cook for another 10 minutes. Leave to cool.

Heat the vegetable oil in a heavy-based pan on medium heat. Add the bay leaves, then, 30 seconds later, the ginger-garlic paste and onions. Cover and cook. When the onions are well glazed, add all the dry spices and cook for 1–2 minutes. Add the matra with any water remaining in the cooker – if none remains, add 70ml (2¼fl oz) – and mix well. Cover and leave to simmer for 10–15 minutes.

Garnish and serve hot with kulchas.

Variation To make pyaaz kulcha, mince 210g (7½oz) onions, 30g (1oz) fresh coriander, and 2 green chillies (optional). Mix in 1 tsp raw mango powder, 10g (¼oz) roasted and ground cumin seeds, and 30g (1oz) salt. Keep for 10 minutes, then squeeze out the water and divide into 6 portions. Knead the dough as for the plain kulcha and divide into 6 portions. Take 1 portion, roll out to about 10cm (4in) and place the onion mix in the centre. Lift the edges to make a pouch, fill with the mix, and seal. Roll out again to 15cm (6in) and bake like a plain kulcha.

Lavasa

A versatile crisp flatbread from the Kashmir region

Makes 6
Prep 40 minutes
Rest 2 hours
Cook 1 hour

1 tsp yeast
350g (12¼oz) maida (all-purpose flour)
1 tsp salt
1 tsp sugar
15ml (½fl oz) ghee

Warm 105ml (3½fl oz) water, add the dry yeast, mix well, and set aside to develop for about 30 minutes.

Set aside 35g (1¼oz) maida in a platter and mix the remaining maida, salt, and sugar in a deep bowl. Slowly add the yeast water while kneading the maida into a pliable dough that does not stick to your hands or the bowl. Coat the dough with ghee and set aside for 2 hours.

Preheat the oven. Knead the dough again till the ghee is absorbed, then divide into 6 equal portions. Take 1 portion of dough and shape it into a smooth ball between your palms. Flatten, turn over in the platter of maida, and roll out evenly to about 23cm (9in) in diameter. Place on a greased baking tray and bake at 180°C (350°F), till the lavasa begins to brown – if your tray is large enough, you can bake more than one lavasa at a time. Serve hot.

Perfect when crisp yet soft.

Naan

Leavened flatbread, which is a staple in traditional north Indian and Mughlai cuisine

Makes 6
Prep 15 minutes
Rest 6 hours
Cook 40–60 minutes

280g (9¾oz) maida (all-purpose flour)
1 tsp salt
1 tsp baking powder
¼ tsp yeast
1 egg
70g (2¼oz) yoghurt (if not using the egg, use an additional 30g/1oz)
15ml (½fl oz) vegetable oil
30ml (1fl oz) ghee

Having set aside 35g (1¼oz) maida in a platter, mix the remaining maida in a deep bowl with salt, baking powder, and yeast. Beat the egg and yoghurt separately, then add these and the oil to the maida and mix well. Slowly add about 35ml (1¼fl oz) water while kneading the maida into a pliable dough that does not stick to your hands or the bowl. Cover and keep for 6 hours for the dough to rise.

Set the oven to preheat. Knead the risen dough again for a few minutes, then divide into 6 equal portions. Cover with a thin muslin cloth while rolling the naans so the dough does not dry out. Take 1 portion of dough and shape into a smooth ball between your palms. Flatten the ball, turn over in the platter of maida, and roll out evenly to about 18cm (7in) in diameter. The typical naan shape can be given by pulling out one side.

Lightly moisten one side of the naan and place this side down on a lightly greased baking tray. If they fit, roll out 3–4 naans, moisten one side, and place them on the tray together. Brush the top lightly with 1 tsp ghee and bake in the oven at 200°C (400°F) until golden-brown spots begin to appear. Take out of the oven and serve hot.

Perfect when light and chewy.

PAIR IT WITH

SIRKA WALE PYAAZ

Place 280g (9¾oz) of peeled, washed, and dried pickling onions, 210ml (7½fl oz) white vinegar, 60g (2oz) sugar, and 10g (¼oz) salt in a clean, dry airtight bottle. Shake well and keep aside for 2 days. Shake a couple of times in between.

Pudina naan

Imbued with the tangy flavours of fresh mint

Makes 6
Prep 15 minutes
Rest 6 hours
Cook 40–60 min

280g (9¾oz) maida (all-purpose flour)
1 tsp salt
1 tsp baking powder
¾ tsp yeast
1 egg
70g (2¼oz) yoghurt (if not using the egg, use an additional 30g/1oz)
15ml (½fl oz) vegetable oil
35ml (1¼fl oz) ghee

For flavouring
30g (1oz) white sesame seeds, roasted
1 tsp raw mango powder
15g (½oz) ginger, finely grated
30g (1oz) fresh coriander, minced
30g (1oz) fresh mint, minced
2 green chillies (optional)

Grind together all the ingredients for flavouring and set aside.

Set aside 35g (1¼oz) of maida in a platter. Place the remaining maida in a deep bowl, mix in the salt, baking powder, and yeast, then add the flavouring, and mix. Beat the egg and yoghurt separately, add these and the oil to the maida, and mix thoroughly. Slowly add about 35ml (1¼fl oz) water while kneading the maida into a pliable dough that does not stick to your hands or the bowl. Cover with a thin muslin cloth and keep for 6 hours for the dough to rise.

Preheat the oven. Knead the risen dough again for a few minutes, then divide into 6 equal portions, and keep them covered so the dough does not dry out. Take 1 portion of dough and roll into a smooth ball between your palms. Flatten the ball, turn over in the platter of maida, and, using a rolling pin, roll out evenly to about 18cm (7in) in diameter. Pull one side to give it the typical naan shape and bake the same way as you would a plain naan (*see p126*)

Perfect when the pudina and raw mango can be tasted.

Lehsuni naan

Brimming with mouthwatering aromas and garlic flavours

Makes 6
Prep 15 minutes
Rest 6 hours
Cook 40–60 min

280g (9¾oz) maida (all-purpose flour)
1½ tsp salt
1 tsp baking powder
¾ tsp yeast
10g (¼oz) red chilli powder
30g (1oz) garlic paste
60g (2oz) onion paste
1 egg
70g (2¼oz) yoghurt (if not using the egg, use an additional 30g/1oz)
30ml (1fl oz) vegetable oil
35ml (1¼fl oz) ghee

Having set aside 35g (1¼oz) maida in a platter, place the remaining maida in a deep bowl and add salt, baking powder, yeast, and red chilli powder. Add the garlic paste and the onion paste, mix well. Beat the egg and yoghurt separately, then add these and the oil to the maida, and mix well once again. Slowly add about 35ml (1¼fl oz) water while kneading the maida into a pliable dough that does not stick to your hands or the bowl. Cover with a thin muslin cloth and keep for 6 hours for the dough to rise.

Preheat the oven. Knead the risen dough again for a few minutes, then divide into 6 equal portions. Remember to keep these covered while rolling the naans so the dough does not dry out. Take 1 portion of dough and roll into a smooth ball between your palms. Flatten the ball, turn over in the platter of maida, and, using a rolling pin, roll out evenly to about 18cm (7in) in diameter. Pull one side to a point to give it the typical naan shape and bake the same way as you would a plain naan (*see p126*).

Perfect when crisp, yet light and chewy.

Paneer naan

A stand-alone bread enveloping a savoury blend of spiced paneer

Makes 6
Prep 45 minutes
Rest 6 hours
Cook 1 hour

350g (12¼oz) maida (all-purpose flour)
1 tsp salt
1 tsp baking powder
¾ tsp yeast
1 egg
70g (2¼oz) yoghurt (if not using the egg, use an additional 30g/1oz)
30ml (1fl oz) vegetable oil
35ml (1¼fl oz) ghee

For stuffing

210g (7½oz) paneer, not set
100g (3½oz) onions, minced
45g (1½oz) fresh coriander, minced
3–4 green chillies, minced (optional)
10g (¼oz) curry powder
1 tsp salt

Knead the dough in the same way as you would for a plain naan *(see p126)*. The primary difference is in the quantity of maida, yeast, and vegetable oil as each naan needs to be thicker to accommodate the filling – so the 6 portions of dough will be bigger.

Place the paneer and all the ingredients for the stuffing in a bowl and hand-mix to a smooth consistency. The mix will be granular but soft. Divide into 6 equal portions and set aside.

Preheat the oven. Take 1 portion of dough and shape into a smooth ball between your palms. Flatten the ball under your fingers, turn over in the platter of maida, and roll out evenly to about 10cm (4in) in diameter. Place 1 portion of the paneer mix in the centre, lift the edges to make a pouch, enclose the mix, and seal the dough pouch. Gently flatten the pouch, turn over in the platter of maida, and roll out to about 18cm (7in) in diameter. Pull one side to a point to give it a typical naan shape and bake as you would a plain naan.

Perfect when crisp outside with a soft creamy filling.

Keema naan

A meat version of the stuffed naan, ideal for a leisurely meal or a quick snack on the go

Makes 6
Prep 45 minutes
Rest 6 hours
Cook 1 hour

350g (12¼oz) maida (all-purpose flour)
1 tsp salt
1 tsp baking powder
¾ tsp yeast
1 egg
70g (2¼oz) yoghurt (if not using the egg, use an additional 30g/1oz)
30ml (1fl oz) vegetable oil
35ml (1¼fl oz) ghee

For stuffing
30g (1oz) fresh coriander, minced
210g (7½oz) chicken, minced
100g (3½oz) onion, minced
15g (½oz) ginger-garlic paste
15g (½oz) garam masala
15g (½oz) coriander powder
10g (¼oz) red chilli powder
¼ tsp turmeric powder
1 tsp cumin powder
1 tsp salt

Prepare this in the same way as paneer naan *(see p130)*: the dough is made as for plain naan – the primary difference being the quantity of maida, yeast, and vegetable oil. The filling needs careful preparation.

Setting aside the fresh coriander, place all the ingredients for the stuffing in a pressure cooker and stir well. Add 140ml (4¾fl oz) water and close the lid and bring to full pressure on medium heat, then leave to cook for another 15 minutes. Allow to cool a little, then take off the lid, and cook on low heat till the water evaporates almost to the point that the mince begins to stick to the bottom. Transfer to a bowl, add the fresh coriander, and mix well to a smooth consistency. Divide into 6 equal portions and set aside to cool.

Set the oven to preheat. Take 1 portion of dough and shape into a smooth ball between your palms. Flatten, turn over in the platter of maida, and roll out evenly to about 10cm (4in) in diameter. Place 1 portion of the keema mix in the centre and carefully lift the edges of the dough to make a pouch, enclose the mix, and firmly seal the mouth. Gently flatten the pouch, turn over in the platter of maida, and roll out to about 18cm (7in) in diameter. Pull one side out to get a typical naan shape and proceed to bake as you would a plain naan *(see p126)*.

Perfect when the keema is moist and flavourful.

Baati, with dal and churma

A traditional speciality from the state of Rajasthan

Makes 6
Prep 30 minutes
Cook 10–15 minutes

350g (12¼oz) atta (whole wheat flour)
1½ tsp salt
1 tsp baking powder
70ml (2¼fl oz) ghee

FOR DAL
45g (1½oz) split chickpea
45g (1½oz) red lentil
45g (1½oz) pigeon pea
45g (1½oz) split green gram
45g (1½oz) split black gram
1½ tsp salt
¼ tsp turmeric powder
30ml (1fl oz) ghee

For tempering
30ml (1fl oz) ghee
10g (¼oz) cumin seeds
2–3 whole red chillies

Mix the atta, salt, and baking powder in a deep bowl before crumbling in 15ml (½fl oz) ghee. Add about 140ml (4¾fl oz) water while kneading the atta into a pliable, non-sticky dough. Cover and keep for 30 minutes.

Set the oven to preheat. Divide the dough into 6 equal portions and keep them covered – a thin muslin cloth works well – while forming the baatis so the dough does not dry out. Take 1 portion and shape into a smooth ball between your palms. Flatten under your fingers and gather up again to form a hollow ball. Make sure to close the top well, and again roll into a smooth ball between your palms. Repeat with the remaining portions.

Place the baati on a greased baking tray and bake at 200°C (400°F) for 10–15 minutes, turning them over and applying a little ghee once in between. The baatis should develop cracks on the surface. Take the baati out of the oven.

To make the dal, mix all the lentils, wash well till the water runs clear, then soak, and set aside for 1 hour.

Drain and place the lentils in a pressure cooker. Add salt, turmeric powder, ghee, and 210ml (7fl oz) of water. Close the lid and bring to full pressure on medium heat, then leave to cook for 7–8 minutes, and set aside to cool.

Heat the ghee for tempering the dal in a heavy-based pan on medium heat, add the cumin seeds. Wait till they splutter, then add whole red chillies and asafoetida powder. When the chillies darken, add the ginger-garlic paste.

1 tsp asafoetida powder
30g (1oz) ginger-garlic paste
35g (1¼oz) onion, chopped
35g (1¼oz) tomato, chopped
1 tsp red chilli powder
1 tsp salt
30g (1oz) fresh coriander, chopped, for garnish

Stir well and cook on medium heat for 30 seconds. Add the onion, sauté till well glazed but not brown, then add the tomatoes and red chilli powder and stir. Cook till you have a masala of even consistency then mix in the lentils and leave to simmer for 2–3 minutes. Garnish with fresh coriander.

Take the baatis, pour about 10ml (¼fl oz) ghee over each one, and serve with dal and churma.

Perfect when turns golden-brown and splits open.

TO MAKE

CHURMA

Take 3-4 baatis and crumble them to a slightly granular texture. Transfer to a bowl, add 45g (1½oz) sugar and 60ml (2fl oz) hot ghee. Mix well and serve with dal and baati. Adjust the sugar to taste – churma should not be too sweet.

Tsot

A breakfast bread from the Kashmir region

Makes 6
Prep 40 minutes
Rest 4 hours
Cook 1 hour

15g (½oz) dry yeast
1¼ tsp sugar
350g (12¼oz) maida (all-purpose flour)
½ tsp salt
1 tsp baking powder
30ml (1fl oz) ghee
15g (½oz) yoghurt
30ml (1fl oz) milk
30g (1oz) poppy seeds

Mix the dry yeast and sugar to 105ml (3½fl oz) of warm water and set aside to develop for about 30 minutes.

Set aside 35g (1¼oz) maida in a platter. Place the remaining maida in a deep bowl, mix in salt and baking powder, then crumble in the ghee and yoghurt. Slowly add the yeast water while kneading a pliable dough that does not stick to your hand or the bowl. Knead the dough for 5 minutes so that it becomes really soft, then coat with ghee, cover, and set aside for 4 hours or till it has risen to double in size.

Preheat the oven. Knead the dough again, then divide into 6 equal portions. Remember to keep the dough covered with a thin muslin cloth while the rolling the tsot so that it does not dry out. Take 1 portion and shape it into a smooth ball between your palms. Flatten the ball, turn it over in the platter of maida, and roll out evenly to about 20cm (8in) in diameter (tsot is thicker than lavasa).

Use the blunt side of the knife, or your fingers, to make long parallel indentations, about 1mm (0.04in) apart, across the centre, leaving a 1cm (½in) border along the edges. Brush the tsot with milk and sprinkle poppy seeds on it.

Place on a preheated tava and cook on low heat for 3–4 minutes on one side only – do turn not turn over. Remove and bake at 180°C (350°F) in a preheated oven for 2–3 minutes till it turns a soft golden-brown. Take out and serve hot.

Perfect when the crust is slightly crisp and the inside chewy.

Litti, with chokha

A stuffed, savoury bread from the state of Bihar

Makes 6
Prep 1 hour
Cook 25–30 minutes

280g (9¾oz) atta (whole wheat flour)
140g (5oz) sooji (semolina flour)
1 tsp salt
1 tsp baking powder
15ml (½fl oz) ghee

For stuffing
140g (5oz) sattu atta (roasted gram flour)
100g (3½oz) onion, minced
45g (1½oz) fresh coriander, minced
15g (½oz) ginger, minced
2–3 green chillies, minced (optional)
1 tsp cumin seeds, roasted and ground
15ml (½fl oz) ghee
1 tsp salt

Mix the flours, salt, and baking powder in a deep bowl, then rub in the ghee. Slowly add about 140ml (4¾fl oz) water while kneading the flours into a pliable, non-sticky dough. Cover with a thin muslin cloth and keep for 30 minutes.

Set the oven to preheat. Place the sattu atta in a bowl, and one by one add all the ingredients for the stuffing, while mixing. Adding the onion will moisten the mix so that it binds when held within a fist. Divide into 6 equal portions and set aside.

To make the littis, divide the dough into 6 equal portions. Make sure they do not dry out while you are rolling the litti by ensuring they remain covered. Take 1 dough ball and pinch it between your fingers and thumb into a small bowl shape. Fill the hollow with 1 portion of the stuffing and gather the mouth of the dough bowl to close it. Then shape the whole into a smooth ball between your palms. When all the littis have been made, place them on a greased baking tray and bake at 200°C (400°F) for 15–20 minutes. They are perfect when golden-brown and crisp.

FOR CHOKHA

250g (8¾oz) eggplant
200g (7oz) tomatoes
15ml (½fl oz) mustard oil
15g (½oz) garlic, minced
100g (3½oz) potato, boiled
100g (3½oz) onion, minced
30g (1oz) green chillies, minced (optional)
45g (1½oz) fresh coriander, minced
10g (¼oz) ginger, minced
30g (1oz) lemon juice
10g (¼oz) salt

To make the chokha, wash and dry the eggplant and tomatoes and lightly rub all over with mustard oil. Score the eggplant in 2–3 places, press the minced garlic into the gashes, then roast on a wire mesh placed over an open flame, turning over regularly so it roasts evenly from all sides. When the skin begins to split, it is done. Set aside. Roast the tomatoes and the boiled potatoes in the same manner but without inserting minced garlic.

Place the eggplant and tomatoes in a large bowl while still hot, pour 70ml (2¼fl oz) of hot water over them, cover, and keep aside for 5 minutes. Take them out of the water, remove the stem of the eggplant, and de-skin all the vegetables. In a shallow dish, first mash the eggplant and tomatoes together, then mash in the potatoes – for an extra tang, you can add a dash of mustard oil 15ml (½fl oz) at this stage. Mix all the other ingredients and set aside.

Lightly crush each litti, pour ghee (to taste) over them, and serve hot with chokha.

Bakarkhani

A soft, flaky sweetbread that traces its origins to the Mughal era

Makes 6
Prep 1 hour
Cook 1 hour

350g (12¼oz) maida (all-purpose flour)
1 tsp salt
10g (¼oz) sugar
1 tsp baking powder
1 tsp green cardamom powder
105ml (3½fl oz) ghee, of which 60ml (2fl oz) is for the dough
165ml (5½fl oz) milk
1½ tsp white poppy seeds

Set aside 35g (1¼oz) maida in a platter and mix the remaining maida, salt, sugar, baking powder, and green cardamom powder in a deep bowl. Crumble in the ghee. Slowly add 105ml (3½fl oz) warm milk while kneading the maida into a pliable dough that does not stick to your hand or the bowl. Knead the dough for an extra 5 minutes, then roll into a large ball. Flatten it under your fingers, turn over in the platter of maida, and roll out evenly as thin as possible.

Spread about 15ml (½fl oz) ghee on the surface and sprinkle some dry maida over it. Fold over both sides, overlaying the edges, carefully spreading 10ml (¼fl oz) ghee over the whole area, fold again. Spread 1 tsp ghee over the length and fold again twice, so that you have a layered square of dough. Cut this neatly into 6 equal portions.

Take 1 portion, shape into a smooth ball between your palms, flatten, and roll into a slightly oval-shaped disc of about 10cm (4in). Do this with each portion, then place them on a greased baking tray. Firmly prick the surface of each bakarkhani with the tines of a fork, but do not make a hole. Brush with 10ml (¼oz) milk and sprinkle ½ tsp white poppy seeds. Bake in a preheated oven at 200°C (400°F) till the bakarkhani are golden-brown. Serve hot.

Perfect when soft and flaky with a crisp crust.

Sheermal

A rich, golden sweetbread brushed with saffron milk

Makes 6
Prep 40 minutes
Rest 2 hours
Cook 1 hour

¼ tsp saffron
70ml (2¼fl oz) milk
350g (12¼oz) maida (all-purpose flour)
½ tsp salt
60g (2oz) sugar
70ml (2¼fl oz) ghee

Soak the saffron in 15ml (½fl oz) milk and set aside.

Set aside 35g (1¼oz) maida in a platter, then in a deep bowl, mix salt and sugar in the remaining maida. Add the ghee and the remaining milk while kneading the maida into a pliable dough that does not stick to your hand or the bowl. Cover and set aside for 2 hours.

Set the oven to preheat. Knead the dough again, then divide into 6 equal portions. To keep the dough from drying as you roll out the sheermal, cover it with a thin muslin cloth. Take 1 portion of dough and shape into a smooth ball between your palms. Flatten, tun over in the platter of maida, and roll out evenly to about 17cm (7in) in diameter – if it seems a little thick, it's because this is a chunky bread. Indent the surface with the tines of a fork at regular intervals.

Place on a greased tray and bake at 200°C (400°F), turning over once or twice in between, till the sheermal turns a nice golden-brown. Brush with the saffron milk and serve hot.

Perfect when soft, flaky, and aromatic.

FRY IN THE KADHAI

Introduction

Puri, the most well-known, deep-fried Indian bread, is not an everyday bread in most homes – it is more likely to be a weekend brunch special and is a definitive festival and celebration special across the length and breadth of the country.

The dough preparation for puris is much the same as for rotis and parathas. The difference being that puris can also be made with a mix of whole wheat and refined flour, or just refined flour. In addition, the dough can be used as soon as it is kneaded and does not necessarily have to be set aside to enhance its elasticity.

As with other breads, a choice of ingredients may be added in the dough. That said, however, there are very few varieties of stuffed puris. The very popular breakfast bedmi (*see p172*) was traditionally a stuffed puri, but today, the ingredients are more often mixed into the flour before kneading – it is also possible to buy pre-mixed, packaged bedmi flour. While there is no doubt that it simplifies the making of a bedmi, it does take away from the authentic flavour.

Once the dough is ready, place the oil to heat in a kadhai while rolling out the puris. There is no standard size for puris – they can be made large or small according to preference. When rolling them out, it is best not to use any dry flour as it can flake off and burn in the oil, potentially giving the puris a burnt appearance and taste. As an alternative, use a drop of oil to prevent the dough from sticking to the work surface while rolling. If, however, rolling puris proves challenging, a small amount of dry flour can be used, but be sure to dust off as much as possible before frying the puri. It is perfectly fine to roll out several puris in advance and set them aside. Once the oil reaches the appropriate temperature, they can be fried quickly in succession, making it easier to prepare a large batch for serving. This efficiency is likely why puris have been, and continue to be, a popular choice for large gatherings.

The kadhai, a deep, inverted, dome-shaped vessel with a broad base that sweeps up to a wide-open mouth, is critical to the process of

deep frying. The shape perfectly complements the function for which it is designed. The concave base, in direct contact with the heat, is where the oil gathers. The deep core therefore, is where the oil is hottest. This is important because a puri will puff up into the characteristic ball-like shape only when it is entirely submerged in hot oil.

This also means that greatest care must be taken to slip the puris into the oil gently and at an angle from the edge of the kadhai to prevent the hot oil from splattering. When slipped in at an angle, the puri will sink to the bottom and drown in the hot oil, cooking quickly before rising slowly to the relatively less hot surface. The wide curvature of the kadhai allows free movement of the long-handled jhara used to flip the puri, brown it to satisfaction, and remove from the hot oil.

Puris remain soft and edible for a longer period as compared to rotis or parathas. To store puris, allow them to cool completely and then place them in an insulated container.

The puri is a weekend brunch special, a definitive festival and celebration special across the length and breadth of the country, and a popular choice for large gatherings.

They can be kept in the refrigerator for up to two days, but should be brought to room temperature before being served. Puris cannot be re-fried or heated in an oven or a microwave as this will cause them to release oil and become unappetizing.

For Indian festivals that require grain-free fasting, puris made from plant-based flours offer a nutritious alternative. Popular options include puris made from kuttu (buckwheat) flour (*see p168*) and singhara (water chestnut) flour (*see pp168–169*). As these flours are generally gluten-free, a binding agent such as potato, is usually used to knead the dough.

Bhatura (*see p176*) is another popular deep-fried bread, especially well-loved in northern India and gradually gaining popularity across the country. Although they are not particularly difficult to make, bhaturas are not commonly prepared at home. Instead, almost every Indian fast food outlet serves them with the traditional pairing of chana. Recent experimentation and innovation have led to exciting versions, including stuffed bhaturas and those with added ingredients in the dough.

Bhaturas are made from refined flour. After kneading the dough, it must be set aside to ferment. Generally, the dough should be left to rise for 3–4 hours if the ambient temperature is around 30°C (85°F) or higher, and for 6 hours if it is cooler.

Once the dough has fermented, kneading it a bit more will make it more pliable and easier to roll out. Unlike puris, bhaturas must be fried individually as they are rolled out. They cannot be rolled and set aside to fry later because the dough tends to shrink if kept. Therefore, it is essential to heat the oil to the right temperature before starting to roll out the bhaturas.

Another unique feature that defines bhaturas and make them a popular fixture at commercial establishments is that they can be fried once and kept aside. At this stage, they are left slightly underdone so that as and when required, they can be re-fried without it turning too brown or looking overdone, and then be served hot and fresh. This is important as bhaturas have to be eaten freshly fried for maximum enjoyment. They cannot be stored or refried a third time. Of course, at home they can be cooked to perfection in the first frying.

Bhaturas and puris aren't the only deep-fried breads made in India. There are a variety of specialties from different regions. The Bengali luchi (*see p162*) is well known, while Madhya Pradesh offers the distinctive Indori palak puri (*see pp170–171*). There is also the babru (*see pp180–181*), from the mountains of Himachal Pradesh, which is rapidly making its way into the heart of India.

Puri, with gholia aloo

Deep-fried bread and a spicy potato curry, perfect for festivals and celebrations

Makes 6
Prep 40 minutes
Cook 12–15 minutes

280g (9¾oz) atta (whole wheat flour)
280ml (9½fl oz) vegetable oil, for frying

FOR GHOLIA ALOO
15ml (½fl oz) vegetable oil
1 tsp cumin seeds
½ tsp asafoetida powder
¼ tsp turmeric powder
1 tsp cumin seeds, roasted and ground
1 tsp red chilli powder
1 tsp salt
280g (9¾oz) potatoes, cut into 2½-cm (1-in) cubes
70g (2¼oz) yoghurt

Use a deep bowl to knead the atta into a pliable non-sticky dough with about 105ml (3½fl oz) water, added slowly. Cover with a thin muslin cloth and keep for 30 minutes.

Divide the dough into 6 equal portions. Keep them covered while rolling the puris, so the dough does not dry out. Take one portion and shape it into a smooth ball between your palms. Flatten gently and roll out evenly to about 15–17cm (6–7in) in diameter. If the dough sticks, smear a touch of oil over the work surface. Roll out all the puris.

Heat the oil on medium heat in heavy-based kadhai – it should not start smoking. If a pinch of dough dropped in the oil floats to the top, it is hot enough. Gently ease the puri into the oil from the edge of the kadhai. When it rises, use a perforated, long-handled spatula to flip it over and cook the other side until golden-brown – this will take only a few seconds. Then remove and drain. The puris are well done when they are puffed up, with one side soft and the other crisp.

To make gholia aloo, heat the oil in a heavy-based pan on medium heat. Add the cumin seeds, when they start to splutter, add all the dry spices and salt, stir, add the potatoes and stir again. Add 350ml (12fl oz) of water and

For garnish

30g (1oz) fresh coriander, chopped

15g (½oz) ginger, julienned

2 green chilles, chopped (optional)

leave to simmer till the potatoes are soft and the water has reduced to half.

Beat the yoghurt to a smooth consistency. Smash the potatoes a bit, turn off the heat, pour in the yoghurt, and mix well. Garnish with fresh coriander, ginger, and green chillies (if using), and serve hot with puris.

Luchi, with panch phoran aloo

A Bengali take on puri and an aromatic, spiced potato medley

Makes 6
Prep 45 minutes
Cook 12–15 minutes

280g (9¾oz) maida (all-purpose flour)
1 tsp salt
¼ tsp sugar
45ml (1½fl oz) ghee
280ml (9½fl oz) vegetable oil, for frying

FOR PANCH PHORAN ALOO
15ml (½fl oz) mustard oil
10g (¼oz) panch phoran masala*
2 whole red chillies
¼ tsp turmeric powder
1 tsp asafoetida powder
1 tsp salt

Place the maida, salt, and sugar in a deep bowl and crumble in the ghee. Warm 105ml (3½fl oz) of water and add slowly while kneading the flour into a pliable dough that does not stick to your hand or the bowl. Cover with a thin muslin cloth and keep for 30 minutes. Knead the dough again – it should be stiff enough to roll without turning in flour – and divide into 6 equal portions. Cover the dough to prevent it drying while rolling the luchi. Take one portion and shape into a smooth ball between the your palms. Flatten and roll out evenly to about 15cm (6in) in diameter. Roll out all the luchi.

Heat the oil in a heavy-based kadhai on medium heat. Test by dropping in a pinch of dough – if it floats to the top, the oil is hot enough. Gently ease one luchi into the oil from the edge of the kadhai. When it rises, use a perforated, long-handled spatula to flip it over and cook the other side until golden-brown. Remove and drain. The luchis are well done when they are incredibly soft.

To make the aloo, heat the mustard oil in a heavy-based pan on medium heat but do not let it reach smoking point,

210g (7½oz) potatoes, cut into 2½-cm (1-in) cubes
1 tsp sugar (optional)

**a combination, in equal proportion, of black mustard, nigella, fenugreek, fennel, and cumin seeds*

add the panch phoran masala. When the masala starts to splutter, add red chillies, the rest of the dry spices and salt. Add the potatoes and stir well. Add 280ml (9½fl oz) of water and cook on low heat for about 15 minutes till the potatoes are soft and the curry thickens. Add the sugar (if using) and adjust the salt if necessary. Serve hot with luchi.

Methi ki puri

Puri infused with fresh fenugreek leaves for additional zest

Makes 6
Prep 1 hour
Cook 12–15 minutes

280g (9¾oz) atta (whole wheat flour)
140g (5oz) fenugreek leaves, minced
10g (¼oz) red chilli powder
10g (¼oz) cumin seeds, roasted and ground
1 tsp salt
280ml (9½fl oz) vegetable oil, for frying

Place the atta, fenugreek leaves, and all the ingredients, except the oil, in a deep bowl and mix well. Slowly add 105ml (3½fl oz) water while kneading the atta into a pliable dough that does not stick to your hand or the bowl. Cover with a thin muslin cloth and keep for 30 minutes.

Divide the dough into 6 equal portions. Cover again while rolling the puris so the dough does not dry out. Take one portion and shape into a smooth ball between your palms. Flatten the ball and roll out evenly to about 15cm (6in) in diameter. Repeat until all the puris are rolled out.

Heat the oil on medium heat in a heavy-based kadhai – it should not be so hot that it starts smoking. Test the oil by dropping in a pinch of dough – if it floats to the top, the oil is hot enough. Gently ease the puri into the oil from the edge of the kadhai. When it rises, use a perforated, long-handled spatula to flip it over and cook the other side until golden-brown. Remove, drain, and serve hot.

Perfect when soft, chewy, and aromatic.

PAIR IT WITH

BOONDI RAITA

Add 1 tsp of salt to 175g (6¼oz) of yoghurt and whisk well. Mix in 35g (1¼oz) minced coriander, and 2 minced green chillies (optional). Add 105g (3½oz) of boondi just before serving, or else it will become soggy. Serve cold.

Singhare ke atte ki puri

Gluten-free puri made from water chestnut flour, traditionally prepared during fasting

Makes 6
Prep 20 minutes
Cook 12–15 minutes

280g (9¾oz) singhara atta (water chestnut flour)
1 tsp raw mango powder
1 tsp salt
100g (3½oz) potatoes, boiled and peeled
30g (1oz) fresh coriander, minced
280ml (9½fl oz) vegetable oil, for frying

Place the singhara atta in a deep bowl, add in the raw mango powder and salt, and mix. Mash the potatoes, rub into the singhara atta, then add the fresh coriander and mix well. Knead and make a pliable dough, so that it does not stick to your hand or the bowl. The potato will act as a binder – do not add water unless absolutely necessary. Divide the dough into 6 equal portions. Cover them with a thin muslin cloth while rolling the puris, so the dough doesn't dry out.

Apply a little oil to your palms and shape 1 portion of dough into a smooth ball. Flatten with your fingers, then pat from palm to palm to extend it as much as possible. This dough will stick while rolling out, so spread a plastic sheet on the work surface and roll out the dough on it to about 13cm (5in) in diameter. Carefully lift the plastic sheet, place with the rolled-out roti face down on a tray, and peel away the plastic. Repeat until all the puris are rolled out.

Heat the oil on medium heat in a heavy-based kadhai. Test by dropping in a pinch of dough – if it floats to the top, the oil is hot enough. Gently ease the puri into the oil from the edge of the kadhai. When it rises, use a perforated, long-handled spatula to flip it over and cook the other side until golden-brown. Remove, drain, and serve hot.

Perfect when soft and crumbly.

Variation To make kuttu ke atte ki puri, take 280g (9¾oz) kuttu atta (buckwheat flour), add 100g (3½oz) boiled potatoes, ¼ tsp turmeric powder, 10g (¼oz) roasted and ground cumin seeds, 1½ tsp salt, 30g (1oz) minced fresh coriander, and 2–3 green chillies (optional). Knead into dough with 120ml (4fl oz) warm water, roll out, and fry the puris, as you would for singhare ke atte ki puri.

Indori puri palak ki

Spinach-flavoured puri from the city of Indore in central India

Makes 6
Prep 25 minutes
Cook 15–20 minutes

420g (14¼oz) spinach, chopped
30g (1oz) yoghurt,
10g (¼oz) ginger, minced
¼ tsp turmeric powder
10g (¼oz) cumin seeds
2 green chillies
30g (1oz) fresh coriander, chopped
280g (9¾oz) atta (whole wheat flour)
1 tsp salt
300ml (10fl oz) vegetable oil, for frying

Having washed, drained, and blanched the spinach, blend it in a mixer-grinder together with yoghurt, ginger, turmeric powder, cumin seeds, green chillies, and fresh coriander – do not add water. Place the atta in a deep bowl, add salt and 15ml (½fl oz) oil, and mix well. Knead the spinach into the atta to make into a pliable, non-sticky dough. Add water only if necessary. Divide the dough into 6 equal portions and cover with a thin muslin cloth so the dough does not dry out while rolling out the puris.

Apply a little oil to your palms, take 1 portion, and shape into a smooth ball. Flatten it, then pat from palm to palm to extend as much as possible, then roll out with a rolling pin to about 15cm (6in) in diameter. Repeat until all the puris are rolled out.

Heat the oil on medium heat in a heavy-based kachai – make sure it does not get so hot that it starts smoking. Test by dropping in a pinch of dough – if it floats to the top, the oil is hot enough. Gently ease the puri into the oil from the edge of the kadhai. When it rises, use a perforated, long-handled spatula to flip it over and cook the other side until golden-brown. Remove, drain, and serve hot.

Perfect when soft on one side, crisp on the other.

PAIR IT WITH

MOOLI LACCHA

Peel and grate 210g (7½oz) white radish in a large bowl. Add 1 tsp roasted and ground cumin seeds, ½ tsp red chilli powder, 1 minced green chilli (optional), 15g (½oz) minced fresh coriander, 30g (1oz) fresh mint, 1 tsp of salt and toss well. Add 30ml (1fl oz) lemon juice, toss again, and serve fresh.

Bedmi, with kaddu

Spiced lentil puri and pumpkin curry, a favourite from Chandni Chowk in Old Delhi

Makes 6
Prep 1 hour
Cook 12–15 minutes

280g (9¾oz) atta (whole wheat flour)
70g (2½oz) maida (all-purpose flour)
310ml (10½fl oz) vegetable oil
¼ tsp turmeric powder
10g (¼oz) red chilli powder
1 tsp asafoetida powder
1 tsp raw mango powder
10g (¼oz) cumin seeds, roasted and ground
1½ tsp salt
105g (3¾oz) skinned black lentil, coarsly ground

FOR KADDU
30ml (1fl oz) vegetable oil
½ tsp fenugreek seeds
1 tsp fennel seeds
1–2 whole red chillies
¼ tsp turmeric powder

Set aside 35g (1¼oz) of atta in a platter and place the remaining flours in a deep bowl. Slowly add about 105ml (3½fl oz) of water while kneading the flours into a pliable, non-sticky dough. Cover and keep for 30 minutes.

Heat 30ml (1fl oz) of oil in a heavy-based pan, add all the dry masalas and salt, stir well, add the skinned black lentils, and stir thoroughly until well mixed. Add 70ml (2¼fl oz) water and cook till the water is fully absorbed and the mix is dry. Allow to cool. Then divide the mix into 6 equal portions.

Divide the dough into 6 equal portions. Cover them with a thin muslin cloth while rolling the bedmi, so that the dough does not dry out. Take 1 portion and shape into a smooth ball between your palms. Flatten and roll out evenly to about 13cm (5in) in diameter. Place a portion of the lentil mix in the centre, lift the edges to make a pouch that encloses the mix, and close the mouth. Gently flatten the pouch and roll out again to about 13cm (5in) in diameter. Repeat until all the bedmi are rolled out. Cover these with the muslin cloth so they do not dry out.

Heat the remaining oil on medium heat in a heavy-based kadhai. Test by dropping in a pinch of dough – if it floats to

1 tsp salt
500g (1lb 2oz) pumpkin, cut into 2½-cm (1-in) cubes
10g (¼oz) raw mango powder
30g (1oz) sugar
15g (½oz) fresh coriander, chopped, for garnish

the top, the oil is hot enough. Gently ease the bedmi into the oil from the edge of the kadhai. When it rises use a perforated, long-handled spatula to flip it over and cook the other side until golden-brown. Remove and drain. The bedmis are well done when they are crispy.

To make kaddu, in a heavy-based pan, heat the oil on medium heat. Reduce the heat and add the fenugreek seeds, fennel seeds, whole red chillies, turmeric powder, and salt. Stir for a few seconds and add the pumpkin. Stir well, cover, and cook for 7–10 minutes, stirring once or twice in between. Add 140ml (4¾fl oz) of water and cook on medium heat for 15 minutes till the pumpkin is soft. Add the raw mango powder and sugar, stir well, and cook for another 5 minutes. Cook, stirring as needed, till the kaddu is a little mushy. Garnish with coriander and serve hot with bedmi.

Bhatura, with chana

Fluffy, deep-fried bread and spiced chickpeas curry, a beloved north Indian combination

Makes 8
Rest 5–6 hours
Prep 45 minutes
Cook 40 minutes

280g (9¾oz) maida (all-purpose flour)
140g (5oz) sooji (semolina flour)
1½ tsp salt
1 tsp baking powder
30g (1oz) yoghurt
310ml (10¼fl oz) vegetable oil

FOR CHANA
140g (5oz) whole chickpeas, soaked overnight
1 tsp cumin seeds
1 tsp salt
30ml (1fl oz) vegetable oil
100g (3½oz) onion, finely chopped
15g (½oz) ginger-garlic paste

Set aside 35g (1¼oz) of maida in a platter and place the remaining maida and all the sooji in a deep bowl. Add salt and baking powder and dry mix the ingredients. Add the yoghurt and 30ml (1fl oz) oil to get a crumbly consistency, then slowly add 105ml (3½fl oz) of water while kneading the flours to a pliable, non-sticky dough. Cover and set aside for 5–6 hours.

Place the remaining oil in a heavy-based kadhai on medium heat. Divide the dough into 8 equal portions. Keep them covered with a thin muslin cloth while rolling out the bhatura so that they do not dry out. Take 1 portion and roll it into a smooth ball between your palms. Flatten and roll out evenly to about 17cm (7in) in diameter.

Test how hot the oil is by dropping in a pinch of dough – if it floats to the top, the oil is hot enough. Gently ease the bhatura into the oil from the edge of the kadhai. When it rises, use a perforated, long-handled spatula to flip it over and cook the other side until golden-brown. Remove and drain. The bhaturas are well done when they are nicely puffed up, but not brown.

To make the chana, drain and place the whole chickpeas in a pressure cooker with the cumin seeds, salt, and 280ml (9½fl oz) of water. Close the lid, bring to

100g (3½oz) tomato, finely chopped
½ tsp turmeric powder
45g (1½oz) coriander powder
10g (¼oz) cumin seeds, roasted and ground
30g (1oz) chana masala
1–2 green chillies, chopped, for garnish
30g (1oz) fresh coriander, chopped, for garnish

full pressure on medium heat, and then allow to cook for another 10 minutes. Take off heat and set aside to cool.

Heat the oil in a heavy-based pan on medium heat, add the onions and ginger-garlic paste, cover, cook for 5 minutes, and then add the tomatoes. Cover and cook again till the mix is well done but not too brown. Add the dry spices and stir well. Add the pressure-cooked chickpeas as well as the liquid left in the cooker. Adjust the salt to taste. Reduce the heat and leave to simmer for 7–8 minutes. The chana should not be watery but thick and soupy; so let the excess water, if any, evaporate.

Garnish with green chillies and fresh coriander and serve with bhaturas.

Variation To make a paneer bhatura, mix 210g (7½oz) paneer, 30g (1oz) minced fresh coriander, 1 tsp each of red chilli powder and roasted and ground cumin seeds 1½ tsp salt to a smooth consistency, and divide into 8 equal portions. Knead the dough and portion it as for plain bhaturas. Roll out each portion to about 13cm (5in) in diameter, lift the edges to make a pouch, fill with one portion of the mix, and seal. Roll out again to about 18cm (7in) and fry.

Babru

A sweet or savoury breakfast bread from the state of Himachal Pradesh

Makes 6–8
Rest 1 hour
Prep 1 hour
Cook 20–25 minutes

210g (7½oz) jaggery
280g (9¾oz) atta (whole wheat flour)
¼ tsp salt
1 tsp baking powder
30g (1oz) yoghurt
1 tsp fennel seeds, crushed
210ml (7fl oz) vegetable oil, for frying

Dissolve the jaggery in 105ml (3½fl oz) of warm water and set aside to cool. Place the atta in a deep bowl, add the salt and baking powder, and mix well. Add the yoghurt and fennel seeds and keep mixing. Slowly add the cooled jaggery water while kneading the atta into a pliable dough that does not stick to your hand or the bowl. Cover and set aside for 1 hour.

Knead the dough once more. Divide the dough into 6–8 equal portions. Cover with a thin muslin cloth while rolling the babru, so the dough does not dry out. Take 1 portion and shape into a smooth ball between your palms. Flatten and roll out evenly to about 10cm (4in) in diameter. Repeat until all the babru are rolled out.

Heat the oil on medium heat in a heavy-based kadhai – test by dropping in a pinch of dough, if it floats to the top, the oil is hot enough. Gently ease the babru into the oil from the edge of the kadhai. When it rises to the top, use a perforated, long-handled spatula to flip it over and cook until golden-brown. Remove and drain. It's best to fry the babru individually unless you have a really big kadhai that will take 2–3 of them together. Serve hot.

Perfect when golden-brown, but soft and chewy inside.

Roth

A sweet bread from the state of Kashmir, shared to celebrate joy and good fortune

Makes 6
Prep 45 minutes
Cook 15–20 minutes

280g (9¾oz) atta (whole wheat flour)
280g (9¾oz) maida (all-purpose flour)
45g (1½oz) sugar, powdered
45g (1½oz) green cardamom seeds, crushed
30ml (1fl oz) ghee
140ml (4¾fl oz) milk
70g (2¼ oz) almonds, crushed
70g (2¼ oz) raisins
30g (1oz) poppy seeds
280ml (9½fl oz) vegetable oil, for frying

Having set aside 35g (1¼oz) of atta in a platter, place the remaining atta and maida in a deep bowl, add the sugar and green cardamom seeds, and crumble in the ghee. Knead to a pliable, non-sticky dough while slowly adding the milk. Cover and set aside for 1 hour.

Divide the dough into 6 equal portions. Remember to cover with a thin muslin cloth while rolling the roth so the dough does not dry out. Take 1 portion and shape into a smooth ball between your palms. Flatten and roll out evenly to about 20cm (8in) in diameter and ½cm (¼in) in thickness. Press in 2 tbsp of almonds and raisins and 1 tsp of poppy seeds onto each roth.

Heat the oil on medium heat in a heavy-based kadhai – not so hot that it starts smoking. Test by dropping in a pinch of dough – if it floats to the top, the oil is hot enough. Gently ease the roth into the oil from the edge of the kadhai and fry until golden-brown. Remove, drain, and serve hot.

Perfect when golden-brown with a cake-like texture.

Glossary

A

aam mango

achar pickle

adrak ginger

aloo potato

anda egg

B

bhari to be filled with

bind the dough kneading warms the strands of gluten present in flour causing them to expand and stick together to form an elastic dough. When kneading gluten-free flour, a binding agent, such as potato, has to be added to form a pliable dough.

boondi small round crunchy chickpea flour fritters that can be plain or salted and spiced.

C

chana chickpea

chapati one of the many names for the roti, phulka, rotli, poli being others. Generally, a chapati is bigger and thicker than a phulka.

chulha an earthen or brick stove that was usually coal or wood fired.

cow dung cakes a mix of cow or buffalo dung, husk, and straw, patted into a thick disc and sun dried. Traditionally burnt as fuel in India.

curry gravy

D

dal pulses or the edible seeds of legumes such as black gram, red lentils, chickpea, kidney beans.

dhania coriander

do palli two layers

G

gajar carrot

gujiya a sweet, deep-fried dumpling traditionally made for Holi festivities.

garam masala a mix of aromatic spices, such as cumin seeds, green cardamom, cinnamon, cloves, black pepper, and nutmeg.

ghee clarified butter

gobi cauliflower

grain-free fasting ritual fast among practicing Hindus during which the consumption of any kind of grain is prohibited, but other foods may be consumed.

H

hari mirch green chilli

J

jolada jowar or sorgum

K

kaddu pumpkin

kamrak starfruit

kathi roll a flatbread wrap filled with meat grilled on a skewer, or a kathi kebab.

keema minced or ground meat, may be either chicken or goat.

keep for cover and set aside to set or develop for a prescribed duration.

khamiri fermented

khira cucumber

L

laccha long, thin slices like shreds.

lehsun garlic

M

makki maize or corn

mandua ragi or finger millet,

matra dried peas

mattar peas

meetha sweet

methi fenugreek

mooli white radish

N

nariyal coconut

nimbu lemon

P

pakke ripe

paneer Indian cottage cheese made by curdling milk.

pakoras fritters

palak spinach

panch phoran masala a combination of five types of whole seeds – black mustard, nigella, fenugreek, fennel and cumin.

Partition the division of the country into India and Pakistan at the time of independence from the British in 1947.

pudina mint

phulka one of the many names for the roti, chapati, rotli, poli, being others. Generally, a phulka is small, sometimes no bigger than the palm of the hand, thin, and light.

pyaaz onion

R

raita yoghurt mixed with vegetables or greens served as an accompaniment to Indian food.

raw mango powder a souring agent.

S

saag leafy green such as spinach and fenugreek.

samosa a triangular, deep-fried pastry case filled with savoury vegetables or meat.

sarson mustard

sattu originally the flour of a combination of seven grains and lentils (*saat anaj*) corn, barley, chickpeas, green gram, pigeon peas, green peas, and horse gram, but now usually only chickpea flour.

Sindhi from Sindh, a province in Pakistan and also the people of Sind, many of whom migrated to India after Partition.

T

tamatar tomato

Y

yoghurt semi-solid dairy product produced by the bacterial fermentation of milk.

Z

zeera cumin

Index

A

B

C

J

K

L

M

N

O

P

Acknowledgments

About the author

Anuradha Ravindranath was born and brought up in Delhi. She inherited her interest in cooking from her late father, Ranjit Rai, who authored *Curry Curry Curry* (Penguin, 1989). This led her to write and publish *Tandoor, the Great Indian Barbecue* (Penguin, 1996) under his name, after his passing. Her book *The Rice Cookbook – 101 simple recipes* (Penguin, 2009) won the Gourmand World Cookbook Award for the best single subject cookbook from India. Anuradha enjoys sharing her love for cooking with enthusiasts of all ages. She has conducted cooking classes for children aged 8 to 12 years for more than 10 years, from 1995 to 2005. She has developed a concept she calls "Survival Cooking" especially for young adults planning to leave home. Her other programmes include workshops, demonstrations, and hands-on experience for international groups with an interest in Indian cuisine; customized visits to local spice, fruit, and vegetable markets; workshops on "De-Stress through cooking"; and cookery demonstrations for schools, colleges and for cultural activities. Anuradha's other lifelong passion has been an enthusiasm and appreciation of pottery.

Author's acknowledgments

I would like to thank MadhuMadhavi Singh, who read the first draft of this book and encouraged me to get it published. Subsequently, she has been a pillar of support and patience, editing it several times until we arrived at the final text.

My sincere thanks to the DK team: Aparna Sharma, who encouraged and supported my effort from the start, Neha Ahuja and Devika Awasthi for the wonderful design, and Chitra Subramanyam and Vatsal Verma for editorial support. I would also like to thank Adhyayan Sahay for bringing the recipes alive and Saumya Gupta for the beautiful photographs.

Special thanks to my husband and daughters, for whom I cooked, and extended and diversified my love for cooking, to my sons-in-law who appreciate everything I put on the dining table, and to my grand-daughters who have brought me immense joy.

Publisher's acknowledgments

The publisher would like to thank Nicobar Design for the tableware and pottery used in the photographs on pages 64, 78–79, 90–91, 101, 103, 134–135, 140–141, 142, 160–161, 166, 170, 178–179; Chandrima Banerjee for editorial input and assistance during the early stages of the book-making process; Shahid Qureshi for editorial support; Shipra Jain, Arshti Narang, and Diya Varma for design support; Harish Aggarwal and Suhita Dharamjit for support in jacket design; Raman Panwar for DTP support; Manpreet Kaur for picture research adminstration support; Shubhdeep Kaur for assistance in photography; and Tathagata Mandal for proofreading.

Disclaimer

Every effort has been made to acknowledge those individuals, organizations, and corporations that have helped with this book and to trace copyright holders. DK apologizes in advance if any omission has occurred. If an omission does come to light, DK will be pleased to insert the appropriate acknowledgment in the subsequent editions of the book.

The publisher would like to thank the following for their kind permission to reproduce their photographs:

(Key: a-above; b-below/bottom; c-centre; f-far; l-left; r-right; t-top)

8-14 Anuradha Ravindranath. **16-17 Dorling Kindersley:** Shubhdeep Kaur. **30 Dreamstime.com:** Bbgum3 (b); Katkaterinara (t). **35 Dreamstime.com:** Sandhyaskitchen. **80 Getty Images:** IndiaPix / IndiaPicture. **86 Alamy Stock Photo:** Sameer Chogale. **111 Dreamstime.com:** Raj Kumar. **116-117 Dreamstime.com:** Kampol Jongmeesuk. **122-123 Dorling Kindersley:** Shubhdeep Kaur. **128 Shutterstock.com:** Hashem Issam Alshanableh. **149 Dorling Kindersley:** Shubhdeep Kaur. **150-151 Dorling Kindersley:** Shubhdeep Kaur. **152 Alamy Stock Photo:** Connect Images / Victoria Zeffert. **154-155 Getty Images / iStock:** mtreasure. **156-157 Alamy Stock Photo:** Photosindia. **164-165 Dorling Kindersley:** Shubhdeep Kaur. **174-175 Dorling Kindersley:** Shubhdeep Kaur

Consulting Editor MadhuMadhavi Singh
Project Editor Vatsal Verma
Senior Editor Suefa Lee
Senior Art Editor Devika Awasthi
Photography Saumya Gupta
Styling Adhyayan Sahay
Jacket Designer Neha Ahuja Chowdhry
DTP Designer Ashok Kumar
DTP Coordinator Tarun Sharma
Pre-Production Manager Balwant Singh
Production Manager Pankaj Sharma
Managing Editor Chitra Subramanyam
Managing Art Editor Neha Ahuja Chowdhry
Consulting Publisher Aparna Sharma

Additional editorial support Rohan Sinha

First published in India in 2025 by
Dorling Kindersley Publishing Private Limited,
208, Ansal's Laxmi Deep
Laxmi Nagar District Centre
New Delhi 110092, India

10 9 8 7 6 5 4 3 2 1
001– 345586–Mar/2025

A CIP catalogue record for this book
is available from the British Library.
ISBN: 978-81-9694-850-4

Printed and bound in China

www.dk.com

MIX
Paper | Supporting responsible forestry
FSC™ C018179
www.fsc.org

This book was made with Forest Stewardship Council™ certified paper – one small step in DK's commitment to a sustainable future.
Learn more at www.dk.com/uk/information/sustainability